URBAN WILDLIFE

URBAN WILDLIFE

Peter Shirley

with illustrations by Steven Kirk

Whittet Books

First published 1996
Text ©1996 by Peter Shirley
Illustrations © 1996 by Steven Kirk
Whittet Books Ltd, 18 Anley Road, London W14 OBY

British Library Cataloguing in Publication Data. A catalogue record for this book is available from the British Library.

ISBN 1 873580 23 1

Printed and bound by Biddles

Contents

Acknowledgments

A book of this nature could not be written without an enormous amount of help from others. Many people have readily given information, advice and encouragement. My thanks to them all, and especially to: Peter Bateman, until recently with Rentokil, Mike Bloxham for information on flies, Roger Broadbent for information from the West Midlands Bird Club, Gerald Dawe of the Urban Ecology Trust for general information, Bob George for advice on fleas, Dr Peter Jarvis of Wolverhampton University for research papers, Tom Langton of Herpetofauna Consultants International for information on lizards, Craig Slawson for information on spiders, and Jim Winsper of West Midlands Bird Club for help with black redstarts.

Indirectly many more people have helped me as I have built up my knowledge of this subject over many years. To all my friends and colleagues I say 'Thank you.' In addition I hope this book stands as a worthy testament to the inspiration given to me and countless others by Max Nicholson and W.G. 'Bunny' Teagle, and to the enormous contribution made in this field by George Barker of English Nature.

In addition I must thank my wife Dot for her patience and assistance and my editor Annabel Whittet for thinking of the book in the first place, inviting me to write it, and being willing to persevere with it.

Peter Shirley MBE

The artist would like to thank Peter Kirk

Preface

By the year 2020 80% of the human race will be living in towns and cities. This means that the vast majority of people will learn about and experience the natural world in an almost entirely artificial environment. The trees, flowers, birds and animals they encounter in their daily lives will be those that can tolerate the often harsh conditions of urban living, or that have had special provision made for them, or that can derive positive benefits from it and consequently succeed where other species may fail.

The ways in which people relate to that wildlife will dictate to a very large extent their attitudes to the natural world in general. These attitudes will be crucial to their understanding of, and willingness to protect, wildlife and its habitats. As these people will wield most of the world's political and economic power, and as the quality of all our lives is dependent upon the health and well-being of the natural world, the relationships will be fundamental to the health of the planet.

It seems strange, therefore, that more attention is not given to understanding the ways in which wildlife thrives and survives in urban areas. There is still a general attitude that 'wildlife' is found only in rural and remote areas, and any that happens to find itself in towns is at best a nuisance, and at worst a dangerous pest. I hope that this book will show that this is not so, and that in Britain we have plenty of opportunities to enjoy, help and protect the rich variety of wildlife just outside our backdoors.

Throughout the book I will use the word 'town' to denote towns, cities and urban areas in general. There is no accepted definition of a 'town', 'city' or an 'urban area'. For our purposes these terms will be taken to mean an area where more than half the land is covered with buildings, roads and other hard surfaces, and where the population density is several thousands of people per square mile.

Introduction

Just under 10,000 years ago people leading semi-nomadic lives in the warm, dry, river valleys of Asia began building permanent settlements. Where there was enough water to support their flocks of sheep and goats and to irrigate the wild grasses they had learned to cultivate, there also was the potential for a settled way of life. Thus it was that in the valleys of great rivers – such as the Yellow River, the Nile, the Tigris and the Euphrates – the social and cultural foundations of today's metropolises were laid down.

One of the earliest recorded great cities was Susa in ancient Persia, which existed in 4000 BC. Other major cities in the region followed, such as Memphis, Thebes, Erech and Babylon. Some ancient cities are enduring very well: for instance, Jerusalem is now about 3,000 years old. Rome is almost as old, having been supposedly founded in 753 BC. Of course many other ancient places have long since disappeared, such as Carthage in North Africa, which is reputed to have had a population of a million people in 800 BC.

In relation to the whole history of the planet towns are, therefore, a new feature in the landscape, and wildlife has had a very short time to learn to exploit this new and strange environment. Side-stepping the dangers and disadvantages of buildings, noise, lights, pollution, continual disturbance and hordes of people and traffic, it has discovered that there are some good things for it in towns. For example there are greatly increased food sources, either in storehouses, gardens, refuse bins or – in modern times – on bird tables. Furthermore this food is available all the year round. Winters are warmer. For some there is comfort and refuge in buildings, so much so that species such as house sparrow, house mouse and house spider are rarely found away from them, and their names serve to indicate how closely associated with humans they are.

All towns share a number of distinct characteristics which enable us to categorise an 'urban habitat'. Unlike 'natural habitats' such as woodland, acid bog, or neutral grassland, the urban habitat has been created as a result of human activity rather than by natural processes. This does not mean that it is devoid of natural features, or is not modified by natural processes. It may be thought of as a mirror image of natural habitats which, whilst retaining their unique characteristics, are heavily modified by human activity. In the case of towns the main habitat is created by human activity and is heavily modified by the natural world.

There is almost always a network of open spaces in towns – such as parks, gardens, wasteland, relic countryside and river valleys. This permeates the built environment and provides homes, refuges and feeding places for plants, animals and birds. This rarely takes up more than one third of the total land area. Approximately half of the rest is taken up with buildings, and the other half with roads, railways, car parks and other paved areas.

red admiral

painted lady

comma

peacock

small tortoiseshell

Exotic Buddleia *attracts native butterflies*

London

'London small and white and clean,
The Thames bordered by its
gardens green.'
– William Morris

'The great wen' – William Cobbett

London is typical of many modern European cities. It has developed on either side of a major river – probably from a crossing point – and has been continuously occupied for more than 2,000 years. Development has sometimes been reversed, for example the Roman brick-built city was destroyed in 851AD and Alfred the Great had it rebuilt in timber. This led to destruction by great fires on at least 5 occasions. Nevertheless the population has generally expanded, especially in the last 200 years. Its modern peak was reached in the middle of this century, and currently the population is declining slightly.

Population of London	
Roman London up to 400AD	50,000
Dark Ages	not known but less than Roman times
13th-15th centuries	40-50,000
1532	62,000
1593	145,000
1665	500,000 (100,000 lost in Plague)
1700	675,000
1801	900,000
1851	2,363,000
1931	9,000,000

Twitchy London

Apparently the capital is the best place in the country to see wild rose-winged parakeets, smew and mandarin ducks. There are even bird watching tours of London, species commonly seen being great spotted woodpeckers, sparrowhawks and great crested grebe.

Towns are generally warmer and drier than the surrounding countryside. There are two main reasons for this. First the bricks and stones of roads and buildings act like giant storage heaters. They absorb the sun's energy during the day and then gradually release it again during the night. Grass, trees and other plants, on the other hand, turn at least part of the same energy into new cells, thus capturing it for a longer period. In addition buildings are often heated, and this artificial source of energy is added to that of the sun.

The higher temperature favours species that need slightly warmer conditions than are normally found in this country. For example *Buddleia* thrives in dry places in British towns. It is a common coloniser of old railway land, demolition sites and crumbling walls. This is no doubt partly due to its liking for lime-rich soil, but even so it has not yet established itself in rural areas.

The second reason is that moisture, whether in the form of rain, dew or mist, unlike energy, is repelled by all of the hard surfaces in towns. Outside the built-up area the soil behaves rather like a sponge, holding moisture before slowly releasing it to the air, watercourses or aquefers. One result of the increased run-off in towns is that natural watercourses are often more polluted than their rural counterparts. Another is the 'spate and trickle' syndrome. This describes the sudden rise in the volume and level of water following rain, and the equally sudden reduction when the water has drained away. Although this is the general position, there is often more standing water in urban areas than in the countryside. This water will be found in places like reservoirs, canals and ornamental pools.

Another important characteristic of towns is their constant state of flux. Buildings and roads are continually being constructed and demolished. Land frequently changes use, for instance from playing field to car park, or from derelict land to business park. Often the change from one type of use to another is abrupt, unlike the gradual changes often seen between one sort of natural habitat and another.

The urban situation favours adaptable species, rather than specialist species which have evolved in association with a stable habitat such as ancient woodland. In general it would be expected that those species which biologists refer to as 'r' strategists would do better than the alternative 'K' strategists (see box on p.12). Typical examples of 'r' strategists are the many short-lived, but often abundant, annual flowers which rapidly colonise newly disturbed ground. Many carnivores are 'K' species, needing good supplies of their prey before being able to colonise an area. People have, in any case, done for most of our native carnivores, species such as the wolf, bear and lynx having been in terminal decline before many of our cities were developed.

Pavel Pysek, an ecologist in the Czech Republic, has studied the diversity of plant life in towns, and concludes that the bigger the city, the more habitats for plants there are. So, for instance, Glasgow, with 0.7 million people, has 1,200 plant species, whereas London, with 7 million people, has over 2,000 plant species. Of course many of these species are not indigenous to the London region, but have been introduced either from other parts of the UK or from abroad.

'K' and 'r' strategists

Scientists studying the ways in which plants and animals reproduce in relation to their environment have described two strategies at opposite ends of a continuum. They call these 'K' and 'r' strategies after symbols used in mathematical formulae applied to the processes involved.

'K' strategists are characterised by slow development, delayed reproduction, large body size, the ability to reproduce more than once in a lifetime and a long life. These characteristics evolve in stable environments with a secure supply of all the resources needed by the species concerned. The species are sometimes called 'equilibrium' species. Their numbers tend to expand until they reach the carrying capacity of their environment. Examples of such species are whales, tigers, crocodiles, eagles and large trees.

'R' strategists are characterised by rapid development, early reproduction, small body size, reproduction only once in a lifetime, but with the production of many seeds or eggs, and a short life. These characteristics evolve in unstable environments with uncertain or intermittent supplies or resources. The species are sometimes called 'opportunist' species waiting for favourable accidents. Examples include many insects, annual 'weeds', orchids and mice and voles.

The distinction is often criticised for it is possible for one species to display both traits under differing circumstances. For example the house mice (see p. 48) in hayricks (an ephemeral environment) are acting like 'r' strategists, but the ones in buildings (a much more stable environment) are acting more like 'K' strategists. Even without such obvious differences in behaviour it may also be difficult to ascribe one or other strategy to a species. As long as it is kept in mind that every degree of variation between the two strategies may be found it is a useful concept to help understand ecological processes.

Although open land is limited in scale, what there is is often not so intensively or harshly managed as agricultural land, providing protection from the gun, hunting dogs and, in modern times, the fatal cocktail of agricultural chemicals.

This new phenomenon of urban living, with its attendant changes to the landscape, local climate and living patterns of people and wildlife, has attracted the attention of scientists who look upon towns in the way that others look upon living organisms. That is to say that the whole system, including the living (biotic) and non-living (abiotoic) parts, the physical structures, the flows in and out of energy, food, materials, and water, is considered as if it were itself some sort of animal or plant. This is the science of urban ecology and its progress will be a significant factor in the way we manage our towns in the future.

The melting pot

Animals have four basic necessities – food, water, shelter and breeding sites. For sedentary species, these all need to be present in the same place, but not necessarily at the same time – hibernation for instance removes the need to find food and water for a period, but places a premium on places to rest and shelter. For mobile species they may be in different places – for example thousands of wildfowl migrate to the British Isles to find winter food, but return to the Arctic to breed. The places that provide these necessities are called habitats.

In this section we will look at wildlife habitats in towns. They fall roughly into two types: those that are related to man-made structures and human activities; and those that are semi-natural and reflect elements of the countryside beyond the town boundary. These divisions need not be mutually exclusive. Gardens and canals, for example, fit comfortably into both.

Artificial habitats mainly consist of buildings and roads, and the provisions made for services, such as sewers, cable ducts and water pipes. The brick, concrete and glass of most buildings are merely surrogate cliffs and rocky outcrops to wildlife. The state of repair dictates how many holes and 'caves' there are for species seeking out such niches. In addition, just as on natural cliffs, vegetation clings to tiny footholds. Lichens, mosses and liverworts adorn walls and paving, ferns, ragworts, grasses, willowherbs and even shrubs and trees such as *Buddleia*, ash and birch are typical of the species that are quick to exploit any opportunities presented by gaps and cracks.

Birds and bats in particular are attracted to buildings for roosting and nesting. Martins and swifts were originally cliff-nesting birds which have benefitted enormously from the expansion of buildings in the landscape. Swallows too have almost certainly increased in numbers as human settlements have expanded. Bats, on the other hand, probably find buildings poor substitutes for their mainly woodland ancestral homes, which have all but disappeared. Without our buildings they would be even worse off. Near the coast birds such as kittiwakes are now colonising tall buildings just as they would tall cliffs. Peregrine falcons in Bristol and Baltimore have adopted roof-tops that precisely mimic their natural nesting places. One of the mainstays of their diet in ages past was the rock dove – and what do they find in city centres? The feral pigeon, descendant of that species!

Small mammals other than bats also find buildings very congenial; many of them are tunnellers and hole dwellers, and find protection and food aplenty in our homes, offices and factories. The domestic cat, tame or feral, no doubt presents some problems, but probably no more than stoats, weasels and owls ever did before buildings appeared. Mice and rats reach parts of our buildings other creatures never reach – cavity walls, gaps beneath floorboards, spaces behind the junk we always meant to clear out, and the holes we make for pipes and cables, are all part of their world.

Even smaller spaces provide happy hunting grounds for a bewildering array of invertebrates. House spiders in the bath pipes, hibernating ladybirds in window frames, ants beneath the larder tiles, slumbering queen wasps in the folds of the spare room curtains – these are just a few examples of the unwitting way in which we play host to often unknown lodgers. The ones we know and love, such as our dogs and cats, often carry their own unwanted guests such as fleas.

Almost anywhere that contains a supply of organic material will have an associated fauna. Wool, leather and cotton clothing attracts moths and other insects, stored food and grain is a banquet for birds, mammals and insects, old paper can be eaten or used as nesting material, timber of all sorts is paradise for wood-boring beetles, and house plants harbour aphids and mites.

The destruction and construction of buildings and other structures provides towns with a unique habitat. This is the empty plot, or 'ruderal habitat'. Typically this has a surface far removed from the underlying soils, consisting of brick and concrete rubble often several feet thick. It provides a generally dry, exposed substrate which attracts very special groups of plants. These will be tolerant of the unusual, and for plants very difficult, conditions, mobile so that they can colonise the site in the first place, and able to complete their development quickly. The sites themselves may only be there for a few months, but new ones are constantly being created. Their fragmentation, the harsh conditions and high levels of disturbance deny many plants and animals the opportunity to establish themselves, but conversely provide others with ideal conditions.

Rosebay willowherb is probably the most prominent of the plants able to take advantage of a fresh plot, but others include ragwort, mugwort, thistles, mayweeds, common toadflax, *Buddleia*, birch, goat willow and ash. With these come insects, and, following them, birds and small mammals to feed on either the insects or the seeds and other plant parts. Predators such as foxes and kestrels complete the web based on what to many would appear to be sites totally inhospitable to wildlife. If they do survive for a few years then delightful tangles of brambles, gorse and nettles, together with grasses, such as couch, Yorkshire fog and cocksfoot, are likely to take them over.

There is no agreement about what to call these plots. 'Wasteland' denies their ecological and other values; 'derelict land' is similarly demeaning, 'open space' is too bland; Richard Mabey would include them in his 'unofficial countryside', Oliver Gilbert at Sheffield University has called them 'urban commons' and others have labelled them 'backlands', 'roughs', 'urban wildernesses' or simply 'wildspace'. For our purposes I will refer to them as 'wildspace'.

The other spaces in between the buildings and roads (that is to say those we use and manage) also play host to a great variety of plants and animals. From the ordered formality of ornamental gardens, with not a leaf or a petal out of place, via churchyards and golf courses to the green acres of relic countryside, our towns usually contain a microcosm of the surrounding countryside. The network of open spaces, formal and informal, holds echoes of our rural past, the substance of

Bat boxes are as good as belfries

our present activities and shadows of its own future.

Typical of the transition from the entirely artificial habitats of buildings to the semi-natural habitats of our countryside are parks and gardens. Here we control nature, making it fit our ideas and follow our patterns. The result in ecological terms is a highly and continually disturbed habitat in which succession – the way in which one sort of habitat changes over time to another sort of habitat, as when wetland dries out and becomes grassland, then scrub and finally woodland – has been eliminated. This does not make the habitat worthless to wildlife. Nectar, fruits and seeds are usually available, if only in limited form; some cover will be provided by shrubs and trees and birds of the woodland edge may be especially favoured by the glade-like structure of many gardens. Water is a common ornamental feature and is the single most valuable element of a creature's needs we can provide. The greater the variety of structure, plant species and management techniques, the more valuable our parks and gardens are for wildlife.

Water in towns almost always has some form of wildlife associated with it. On occasions this may only be the green algae which many think disfigures ornamental pools in our squares and plazas. Plants and animals are opportunistic however and have to take their chances where they can. Water is generally in short supply in towns, so where it does appear it is very valuable. Natural watercourses are often polluted, culverted and deprived of their natural banks, washlands and con-

Many bridges provide roosts for bats

tours. Ironically artificial water bodies, such as canals, reservoirs, old gravel pits, flashes and park pools are often more valuable for wildlife.

Canals are particularly noteworthy, both as wildlife habitats and as features in the urban landscape. They look like rivers, but ecologically are like ponds. Their slow-moving shallow water favours pond life – plants such as fennel pondweed, animals like whirligig beetles and pond skaters, frogs and coarse fish, water voles and moorhens. Their long, thin shape provides an enormous amount of edge habitat in relation to the surface area of the water. This is ideal for such things as water mint, yellow flag, reed sweet-grass, water dock and hemlock water dropwort. If many of our urban conurbations can be described as 'endless villages' (as Bunny Teagle once described the Black Country in the West Midlands) then our canals may be called the 'endless village ponds'.

The reservoirs that feed the canals and those that hold our domestic water supply, together with small lakes and pools in parks and large gardens, provide another rich source of generally clean water. Their value for wildlife depends very much on their surrounds, and especially on the way in which their perimeter is managed. Edges that imitate natural shore lines, with gentle gradients, contours and emergent vegetation, will be rich in wildlife. Harsh, hard, concrete rims, close mown grass and paved footpaths to the water's edge will severely limit the opportunities for plants and wildlife to make a living. Even so such pools may still provide resting and feeding places for waterfowl, a home for fish, sufficient gnats and mosquitoes to feed bats and swallows, and a source of drinking water for passing foxes.

Another significant habitat is **grassland**. Globally steppes, savannahs, pampas and other grasslands take up one third of the planet's land area. In the United Kingdom centuries of woodland clearance and grazing have made it our most abundant habitat. In towns great swathes of close mown grass sweep across our parks and other open spaces. The energy expended in maintaining these areas produces another highly stressed, but in this case species poor, habitat.

These circumstances, which mitigate against diversity, do favour a small number of plants that can tolerate the conditions. Typically these will be rosette-forming or low-growing species like daisies, dandelions, speedwells, clovers and – on old grassland rather than seeded grassland – bird's-foot-trefoil. When grass cuttings are not collected these sites become rich in nutrients and without mowing would favour such plants as nettles and cow parsley.

Some of the wildspace mentioned earlier provides official and unofficial grazing land, usually for ponies and tatter's horses. Grazing produces a different effect to mowing. This is because mowers are indiscriminate destroyers, but animals are choosy about which species they eat and which they leave alone. In addition horses leave some parts of their paddock ungrazed, usually areas where they defecate. Grazed paddocks are often adorned by ragwort and thistles and strange mutated shrubs browsed into a sort of equine topiary, which, although different in every paddock, are immediately recognisable. Other town grasslands include old farmland, the grasses colonising older wildspaces, steep hillsides, road, railway and canal verges, golf courses and playing fields (the playing fields often as much plantain as grass), the clipped and striped lawns of suburbia and occasionally washlands for rivers. Collectively they provide a fragmented but wide range of sites, varying in size, ecological characteristics and land-use. They are nearly all managed or used in some way which prevents succession to scrub and woodland.

If grassland is fragmented and varied in towns, then **woodland** is positively atomised. For the most part it consists of tiny slivers of once extensive forests, mature, even-aged plantations between 50 and 250 years old, young plantations created since the end of the war, even younger small, dense stands of amenity and conservation plantings less than 20 years old and semi-natural woodland on unmanaged wildspaces. Because even small groups of trees are prominent in the landscape it is easy to over-estimate the amount of woodland in our towns. In the West Midlands woodland occupies just over 2% of the land area, and of this ancient woodland only a paltry 0.5%. In Greater London woodland covers about 4.5% of the land, and in Newport, Gwent, less than 4%. The value of any woodland to wildlife depends upon a number of inter-related factors: the age of the

percentages of typical habitats in urban areas				
habitat	London Borough of Lewisham	London Borough of Barnet	Newport (Gwent)	Birmingham and the Black Country
broad-leaved-woodland	2.5	3.8	3.82	2.17
scrub	0.5	1.5	0.97	3.31
unimproved grassland	3.0	10.5	0.01	NA
ruderal	0.5	.75	6.12	0.59
standing water	0.1	0.4	0.25	0.92
running water	0.2	0.8	0.4	NA
parkland and improved grassland	3.5	7	4.53	NA
arable and bare ground	0.2	0.75	NA	NA

This table is indicative only of the relative lack of various habitats: the information should not be taken as accurate.

trees (and whether they are all the same age or, which is preferable, of different ages); the number of species (the greater the diversity, the greater the value); the area; the physical structure; and the way in which the woodland is managed and used.

Almost all town woods are secondary – that is, they have developed since the original woodland in the area was cleared – but some of them are on sites which

IT'S A WONDERFUL LIFE

have a history of continuous woodland cover stretching back for several centuries. These are likely to be the best for wildlife. They will probably shelter native woodland flowers, such as lesser celandine, dog's mercury and bluebells. In addition, they will probably have a wide variety of shrubs and small trees, be physically and structurally diverse – with good soil structure, leaf litter, ground flora, understorey, high canopy, standing and fallen dead and dying timber, wound scars, holes and hollows in living trees – and have features retained from previous management such as old coppice stools, pollards and boundary banks and ditches.

The opposite is more likely to be the case in the many small regimented plantations of mainly exotic conifers, with all damaged or fallen timber cleaned out and virtually no ground flora or understorey.

As well as woodlands, the town tree stock includes millions of individual trees growing in streets, parks, cemeteries, churchyards and gardens. These provide mini-habitats giving food and shelter to many creatures. The management of town trees is being increasingly approached through the concept of urban forestry. This involves looking at all the trees in a town – for instance in gardens, parks, woodlands and plantations as you would the trees in a forest. Each of them has its place, and may or may not be suitable for where it is growing. Gradually the tree stock can be added to, unsuitable trees can be replaced with more suitable specimens – for example small trees rather than forest giants in small gardens, and people can get involved in the process through becoming tree wardens, or by joining conservation schemes. Woodlands can be managed rather than neglected, the sides of roads and railways can be planted up, vacant land can have perimeter planting, and eyesores can be screened. Contractors who have to lay cables or pipes can be offered codes of practice which protect tree roots from damage. Schools and others can grow trees using seeds from the existing stock.

Trees, either as individuals or as woodlands, are probably the most loved of all natural features. People remember and value the bluebell woods of their childhoods, the large tree on the corner of their road, their favourite garden tree or the trees they planted as schoolchildren in the corners of the local playing fields. Perhaps it is collective guilty conscience related to the fact that the more humans prosper the more damage is done to the world's trees, but they occupy a very special place in people's affections.

As well as the major habitats, all towns contain a number of smaller even more fragmented habitats. These may be semi-natural, such as heathland, marshland or bog, or almost entirely artificial like sewage works, mineral dumps, disused quarries and refuse tips. Frequently there is a combination of features – for example a large cemetery near to Birmingham city centre was previously a sandstone quarry.

Finally we have to take account of a common physical feature which may encompass different habitats – the corridor. This is an area of more or less continuous open space, often associated with other functions such as roads and railways, along which plants and animals may disperse. They are valuable elements within the urban landscape, helping to loosen the fabric and providing people with the opportunities to enjoy wildlife wherever they weave their way past our offices, shops and homes. An example of the usefulness of these corridors was provided in London's Gunnersbury reserve, where a muntjac appeared in March 1995; its hoofprints were still around at the end of the month. It is assumed that it made its way there by the railway. Muntjac are increasing in the outer London suburbs and are now said to visit every public park in Birmingham.

Do London muntjac travel by rail?

The green mantle

The semi-natural habitats mentioned in the last section form a soft green mantle, cocooning the harsh and hard buildings of towns. The mantle is woven from hundreds of species covering the whole range of the plant kingdom. Lichens cling to buildings and footpaths, ferns, mosses and liverworts huddle in damp places, grasses seek the breezes that carry their pollen, flowers bloom wherever they can gain a roothold, and trees march in single file or small platoons across the urban landscape. This greenery helps to bring nature into the heart of our cities by providing the food and living quarters for many species of animal, bird and insect.

Plants in towns will have arrived in one of five ways: from species there before development took place; from pioneer species with mobile seeds able to colonise bare ground; from introduced or cultivated species used as ornamental plants in parks and gardens; from introduced or cultivated species used for food, medicine or other purposes; from stowaways travelling in vehicles, clothes and goods. As always these categories are not mutually exclusive.

The mechanisms of evolution are such that there are thousands of species of plant occurring naturally in the northern and southern temperate zones of the world which, once transported here, are able to thrive. Our geographical isolation (in that Britain became an island soon after the last ice age) means that initially relatively few plants flourished here compared to mainland Europe. On the other hand our more recent military and commercial history has resulted in a continuous succession of new arrivals. The mildness of our climate (which is enhanced in towns) has helped many of them to establish themselves. Many are now part of our natural history.

Our exotic guests include familiar large trees such as sycamore, horse chestnut and false acacia (from mainland Europe, the Balkans and North America respectively). Less prominent species may be discovered almost anywhere. For instance evening primrose from North America, summer-cypress from Asia (not a cypress at all but a goosefoot!), toothpick-plant from the Mediterranean area, canary-grass from north-west Africa and the Canary Isles, and fox-tail bristle grass from China.

Even a very small site, such as a town garden, can contain a cosmopolitan array of plants. *Mahonia* from the Pacific coast of North America may rub shoulders with *Hebe* from New Zealand. Beneath them South African Livingstone daisies may consort with their English cousins such as ox-eye daisies or feverfew. Pampas grasses from South America could lord it over our more modest Yorkshire fog or meadow grass, and an untended bare patch may see north-east Asian pineapple mayweed competing with Italian 'Oxford' ragwort.

Less disturbed places will usually contain a higher proportion of the plants naturally occurring in the area. Canal, railway and river banks are good places

Cinnabar moth caterpillars on ragwort

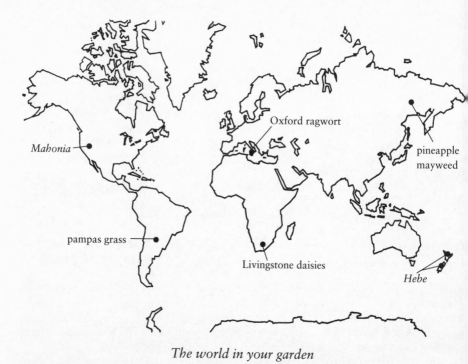

The world in your garden

for these relic species. Towns built on heathland will have heather, wavy hair-grass, gorse and broom appearing in many places. Old woods are often carpeted with bluebells, lesser celandine and dog's mercury, and old grasslands may contain adder's-tongue fern or field scabious. Wet areas are often rich in orchids, lady's smock, ragged robin and meadowsweet.

Plants provide many clues to previous agriculture and industry. Alfalfa or lu-cerne is a member of the pea family once grown for fodder, but now restricted to odd plants surviving in obscure corners. Old oaks growing in areas where there is a leather industry, such as Walsall in the West Midlands, may have originally been planted to supply bark for tanning. Small reed beds could be all that remain of larger areas grown for thatching.

In any individual garden, park or other open space there is probably a unique group of plants, not precisely replicated anywhere else. The soil or other substrate, climate, degree of disturbance and land-use history will combine to dictate the species composition of the site. The local wildlife will be left to make of it what it can. Generally speaking the greater the proportion of native species the better off the wildlife will be. This is not to say that exotic species are of no value to wildlife, merely that they will usually be of less value. On the other hand a small site which contains a mixture of species from every continent – such as a garden – will probably support a greater variety of wildlife than a larger site with just a few native species – such as a reed bed.

Some plants arrive in our towns with all the attributes needed for success. Oxford ragwort hails from the bare, sun-scorched slopes of volcanoes in southern Europe. It is one of about 2,000 species in the genus *Senecio* (the largest genus of flowering plants in the world), some others of which are trees growing at high altitudes on African volcanoes. This family background makes it an ideal coloniser of old walls and rubble-strewn sites which mimic the conditions back home – dry, well drained and exposed. All it has to do is get its seeds into cracks and crevices. Here again it is well equipped. It produces lots of seeds, each with its own parachute which wafts it away on the slightest breeze.

Another very successful exotic is touch-me-not (also called policeman's helmet or Himalayan balsam). This stout annual shares a common characteristic with many other annuals in that its seeds are despatched to distant places to seek the bare ground they need to germinate. There are two parts to the distribution process. First the seed pods explode (often when touched, hence the name) scattering the seeds several feet away from the parent plant. This may not appear to achieve very much, but the plants grow near to water and the seeds float. Enough of them are ejected into or close to water to enable the second part of the process to take place. We have already seen that urban watercourses have widely varying flows. The seeds wait for the next flood, are picked up and carried away, and then deposited on the bare banks as the water goes down again. The rising and falling water also scours the banks and so helps to provide the bare patches needed.

Not all of the plants pre-adapted for life in modern towns are exotic. A group of native plants which find town life to their liking are scurvy grasses. These are tiny members of the cabbage family found on saltmarshes around our coasts and estuaries. At first sight saltmarshes seem to have nothing in common with urban areas, but in this case the common factor is salt. The amount of salt put on our main roads in the winter is sufficient to create the right soil conditions for scurvy grasses to thrive. They are now found on central reservations and roadside verges throughout the country, including in the heart of the West Midlands – about as far from the coast as you can be in Britain.

There is one group helping to weave the green mantle whose members are superficially very well suited to be city slickers. These are the lichens. Strictly speaking these are not plants but composite organisms consisting of an alga and a fungus living together. Their natural habitats include bare earth and rock surfaces, and so the walls and pavements of towns should provide them with unlimited living quarters. Their ability to take advantage of this is limited however because they cannot tolerate air pollution. Here is an example of a group which cannot achieve its full potential in what appear ideal conditions. We utilise this sensitivity to help to assess air pollution, and the success of our efforts to combat it. Following the sharp decline of town centre lichens in the last two centuries some are now making a slow comeback as the quality of air improves.

Although not really part of the green mantle, it is appropriate to mention fungi in this section. Fungi are the third group of multi-cellular organisms (plants and animals are the other two) which make up the bulk of the natural world as we experience it. Unlike plants, which use sunlight to generate the energy to turn inorganic materials into living tissue, fungi are nourished by organic matter, rather as animals are.

Toadstools, mushrooms and moulds all reproduce by means of microscopic spores and for this reason may turn up anywhere that provides the right food for them. Urban conditions favour them in a general way by providing many places for spores to germinate. The constant disturbance, the presence of many plants growing in less than ideal conditions (and therefore offering less resistance to attack), damaged or lopped trees and shrubs, organic detritus (such as discarded food, compost heaps and piles of waste) and the timber and other natural materials used in buildings and artefacts, all contribute to their opportunities.

Fungi are a major factor in the processes of decay and recycling. Without them we would by now be buried under our own rubbish and waste. Despite their all-pervading presence many species are never seen by people at all. Even the most familiar, such as the brilliant red fly agaric, puffballs and mushrooms, are invisible for most of the year. They mainly consist of fine threads, called 'mycellium', which spread throughout, and are hidden in, their organic host. The 'toadstool' is only seen for a few days or weeks and is the fungal equivalent of a flower. It appears only to produce and launch the spores.

There is no evidence of fungi adapting to urban conditions in any way. They will, however, take any opportunities offered, and a study in the Polish city of Lodz discovered that there were more species of fungi in the city than species of plants. It may be that similar studies in rural and remote areas would produce similar results.

Martens *v.* motorists

In 1979 motorists in Winterthur in Switzerland began to complain of vandals damaging their car engines. When the culprits were discovered at work, gnawing ignition cables and coolant hoses, they turned out to be stone martens (more cosmopolitan relatives of our pine martens). Audi reckoned that 10,000 of its customers were victimised by stone martens every year. Stone martens have taken to the urban environment, and in particular the car. The reason seems to be that – unlike pine martens – stone martens don't have fixed habitats or food preferences, and therefore will explore, when young, the food potential of anything, including the automobile. Nor is it just cars – martens are partial to electric cables of all kinds and one in Austria managed to link up live wires in a power station which left 25,000 people without electricity for 2 days!

The inhabitants

BADGERS

Badgers are the largest carnivores in Britain. They are related to dogs and bears, and like dogs have a very good sense of smell. Their closest relatives are weasels, stoats, otters and martens, with which and other species they make up the Mustelid family. They are present in many towns, but usually because the town has reached out to them, rather than because they have 'moved in'. This is illustrated by the number of places that are named after them – for example Brocton, Brockholes, Brockhurst and Brockhampton.

Even though they are classified as carnivores, badgers eat many things. They are gatherers rather than hunters. Earthworms are their favourite dish, but they also take carrion, insects, small mammals and birds, fruit, vegetables and seeds. They will dig out ant, wasp and bee nests – eating the adults, grubs, pupae and honeycombs – root underneath cow pats, scrape bark off trees to get at the insects beneath, and scavenge along road verges. Their catholic taste in food leads them to try all sorts of things, some of them dangerous. For example they have been seen crunching glass bottles and chewing golf balls! They can uncurl and eat hedgehogs. Badgers may be attracted to gardens by putting out a mixture of food. One householder has succeeded in attracting up to 16 badgers at once to her patio banquet, whilst another has saved her local badgers the trouble of digging out bees' nests by making them honey sandwiches.

Although they have no natural enemies and may live up to 14 years, many badgers die young – up to two thirds of cubs die in their first year, and about one third of all adult badgers die each year. The main culprits, sometimes unwittingly, are people. We no longer kill badgers for their meat or fur (badger hams were once eaten in Ireland, and their fur was used amongst other things for shaving and artists' brushes, and for the best sporrans) but deliberate killing still takes place. Road accidents also account for many deaths. In 1984 a survey revealed that 984 badgers were killed on the roads in southern England.

Badgers have been here for nearly two million years and have only had to cope with urban life for the last few hundred of these. At the turn of the century they were scarce, probably because of disturbance and persecution. They are now considered to be abundant. This expansion of the population has taken place at the same time as the expansion of many towns, and has not stopped them moving away from city centres. For example the famous sett at Kenwood on Hampstead Heath, which was occupied earlier this century, has now gone. Copenhagen's badger population reduced by a third from 1975 to 1985, and this is thought to be as a result of disturbance rather than habitat loss.

Badgers' needs for open space and seclusion, and their lack of flexibility ex-

Badgers may continue to live in areas after houses are built

cept in the matter of food, makes it difficult for them to move into towns, but this is balanced against the imperative to establish new territories and their stick-in-the-mud habits. The latter means that an existing group may well continue to occupy their territory after houses and roads have been built around and in it. People providing food will help them to thrive, because like most animals they will expend the least energy possible in feeding. In addition they need to lay down fat reserves for the lean winter months. This is particularly important for the sows that will be bearing litters of cubs. The group will be in trouble however if there are no ways for young animals to leave and join them. In a natural environment the youngsters (especially boars) would leave the family group; if they cannot, they will eventually be ostracised and will probably die young as a result. If no young animals can join the group, it will be at risk from genetic isolation.

Badgers are helped to face these problems by legislation. It is illegal to kill, take or disturb them, or to destroy or block their setts, unless you have a licence.

These may be issued for a variety of reasons, but in towns they will usually be linked to planning permission to build on land containing a sett. In these circumstances killing of badgers will not be permitted, but occasionally moving them to another area may be. English Nature, the agency that issues licences, will expect any activities affecting badgers to be carried out between July and November to avoid disturbing animals in the breeding season. People applying for licences have to show that they have a lawful reason for doing so, and have to comply with a rigorous set of conditions and guidelines.

Many people welcome the prospect of badgers visiting their gardens or allotments, whilst others view it with alarm and despondency. Their enthusiasm for fruit and vegetables, their habit of digging, whether for food, latrine pits or setts, and the physical damage they can do whilst moving around, do not endear them to everyone. As the badger population expands it is likely that more householders, especially those near to the edges of towns and large open areas within towns, may be subjected to the delight or despair of finding badgers in their gardens. The setts those badgers occupy are likely to be in quiet woods and parks and other relatively secluded places, such as the grounds of institutions like colleges and hospitals. Railway and other embankments sometimes offer ideal sett-building sites, but these are no good without adjacent foraging areas.

It seems that although townspeople and badgers have had little to do with each other for the last hundred years they may be about to be reacquainted. How brock's nocturnal lumberings will fit in with 21st century human lifestyles remains to be seen.

Badger befrienders

Brock is no different from any other animal when he can find easy meals. Because of this there are frequent reports of badgers that live close to houses becoming tame after regular feeding by householders. In one famous case the lady concerned was quite happy to share her living room with up to a dozen badgers every night. This may seem like wildlife heaven to some people but it is a dangerous activity to indulge in. Like so many other things, it is more difficult to stop than to start (assuming you have some local badgers).

The animals become used to the fireside fast food, and will persist in arriving at the usual time even if the restaurant is not open for some reason. They may vent their frustration by going on the rampage round the neighbourhood – rather like spoilt children denied their sweets. Their health may suffer if they are not eating a natural diet as a result of being provided for, and young animals may never learn to forage for themselves.

If you want to help the badgers in your neighbourhood leave them to get on with their lives in the ways that suit them best, and help your local badger group or wildlife conservation trust who are probably fighting the badgers' case against developers and road builders.

BATS

Bats are twilight creatures. Their ghostly flight in the half light of dawn and dusk, and apparent disappearance at all other times, has endowed them with sinister mystery. As a result they have suffered undeserved persecution and slander. They are in fact unobtrusive and inoffensive animals whose impact on people is almost always good. The few species flying over our city streets today are the urban descendants of essentially woodland creatures whose ancestors graced the skies 60 million years ago.

There are about a thousand species of bats in the world – only rodents amongst the mammals have more. One of the bats has a good claim to being the smallest of all mammals. It is the 'bumblebee' bat of Thailand and is about the size of a 1p coin. Fourteen species live in Britain. Two – pipistrelle and brown long-eared – are commonly found in and around houses. Of the others serotine bats are the most likely to be found in dwellings, especially in the south-east. These three species account for well over 80% of all bats found in houses in this country.

The myths and legends about bats are often fantastic but usually far from the truth. Just to put some parts of the record right: bats generally have good eyesight, they will not become entangled in your hair, they are mainly brown and grey, not black, and they prefer to roost in modern clean houses not dusty draughty old ones. The truth about bats can be more bizarre then the legends. For instance our brown long-eared bat has the longest ears relative to its body size of any mammal, and some species may spend more than 90% of their lives sleeping.

Long ears are part of many bats' echo-location system. It is possible to see this in action. Find a regular haunt of bats, such as a river or canal, and position yourself beneath their flight path. Wrap a pebble in a piece of cloth. When the bats start patrolling throw the pebble into the air. The bats will be seen to swerve towards it. It is alleged that sometimes they will follow the pebble back down to the ground, but I have not seen them do this.

Because of the great decline in bat numbers this century all British bats are now protected by law from killing, taking and disturbance. If you discover a bat roost in your house you must take expert advice before treating roof timbers or trying to evict the bats. Most of the 'problems' you may anticipate will not materialise. Many roosts are temporary and hold only a few bats. They do not smell or make a lot of noise (some people can hear bat squeaks) and their droppings are dry and odour-free. The wrong action can result in great problems for both householder and bats. One famous case involved a nursery roost in a roof space. The owner saw where the bats were entering and leaving, and blocked this access point when most of the bats were out. This was at the time when the baby bats were too big to be carried by their mothers. When the mother bats returned they made frantic efforts to get back into the roof and ended up flying around inside the house.

Bats in houses are usually so unobtrusive that no one knows they are there. I know of one householder who has a famous wildlife garden, and works hard to attract birds, frogs, newts and foxes. It was only when a neighbour mentioned the bats flying in and out of the roof space that their presence was revealed. If those bats were pipistrelles then they would probably be roosting in tiny spaces behind boards and slates. If they were brown long-eared bats they would more likely be found clinging to the ridge boards.

One of the many problems that bats have faced in recent times has been the treatment of roof timbers with poisons used to kill wood boring beetles. Bats clinging to treated timbers months or years after the poisons were applied have also been poisoned and died. Many of the original products have now been replaced, and it is in any case illegal to use chemicals known to harm bats. This is not just a case of being nice to bats – like them we are mammals; if the poisons affect them they are also likely to affect us. We should perhaps be grateful for the bats' sacrifice.

Even though some people seem to be willing to go to any lengths to rid themselves of wildlife, whether bats or not, some seem to make up for this with an extraordinary amount of tolerance. The build up of bat droppings (guano) beneath a serotine roost in a roof space once caused a ceiling to collapse on to the unfortunate householder who was taking a bath. Despite the sudden shower of laths, plaster and guano this person was perfectly happy to allow the bats to continue sharing her house.

All British bats are insect eaters (other bats eat fruit, fish, frogs, small rodents and

serotine bat

long-eared bat

pipistrelle bat

birds, and even other bats) which means that there is virtually no food for them in the winter. As with other insect eaters, they have to do one of two things – migrate or hibernate. Swifts and swallows migrate, hedgehogs and bats hibernate. Individual bats will wake up from time to time through the winter and may be seen flying, and others will be disturbed and may move around in the roost, or find a new roost Generally speaking, though, bats are not active from October to April.

Pipistrelles, the smallest British bats, are between 3 and 5 centimetres (1 and 2 in.) long (excluding their tails which are about 3 centimetres). Their weight varies from about 3 to about 8 grams, depending upon the time of year. They have a wing span of about 20 centimetres (8 in.). Long-eared bats have a similar sized body, but their longer tails (up to 5 centimetres) and huge ears make them appear much larger. They weigh between five and ten grams.

Most of the animals that are successful in towns are unspecialised and adaptable. The bat – or reremouse or flittermouse – is different. It has a very particular lifestyle, its food is limited and its accommodation needs are exacting. Houses and other buildings make reasonable substitutes for caves, and the amount of open water helps to provide the millions of insects needed. (One pipistrelle may eat 3,000 small insects each night.) Canals are especially good for bats, the water is home to mosquitoes and gnats, and bridges and other canalside buildings provide roosting sites. The waste food in towns which foxes and squirrels eat is of no direct help to bats, although it may provide breeding and feeding places for insects. Parks and gardens provide good hunting grounds amongst the trees, and these places echo the bats' woodland origins. On the other hand predators abound. Domestic cats are responsible for the deaths of many bats, and rats, stoats and weasels are capable of getting into roofs and other places and destroying colonies of bats. Tawny, little and barn owls will all take bats. Magpies have been known to position themselves at the entrances to roosts and to snap up the bats as they emerge. It may be that the poisoning of their roosts was one problem too many, and that now that it has stopped (or should have done) urban bat populations will either stabilise or increase.

We can help bats to thrive by increasing and improving the accommodation available to them. Bat boxes are as easily available as bird boxes, although their occupation is much more uncertain. Even so it is worth putting up some bat boxes to help the bats in your neighbourhood (and as many as 65 bats have been found in one box). Special tiles and 'bat flaps' can be attached to buildings to allow them easy access. In Texas early this century bat towers – a type of super bat box – became fashionable. They were intended to attract bats in sufficient numbers to make inroads into the mosquito population and also to provide bat droppings, or guano. This is a much prized fertiliser, which in some parts of the world is gathered for sale from bat caves. In 1917 a bat protection law – perhaps the first in the world – was passed in Texas.

Feeding bats directly is not a practicable proposition, but reducing the use of insecticides in your garden and building a pond may help to increase their insect food. Perhaps it is most important not to let your, or other peoples', fascination for bats lead to disturbance of roosts. What bats need is peace and quiet, to get on with what for them is the serious business of sleeping.

RED FOXES

Today the animal that most symbolises wildlife in the city is the red fox. For thousands of years foxes have lived alongside people, never dependent upon them, never wholly accepted and trusted, but always there, and often given grudging respect. As towns and cities grew so foxes learnt to exploit the new habitat. They gatecrashed our suburban garden party – and stayed.

This should not surprise us. Foxes are not at all fussy about where they live or what they eat. In the UK they can live anywhere, from saltmarshes and sand dunes to the tops of our highest mountains. They eat almost anything that comes their way, whether it be shellfish and crabs, fish, insects, worms, mice, rabbits,

Foxes seem to have taken to towns and cities

birds or discarded burgers and chips. They are willing to travel for good meals; exact distances vary according to the area they are in, but town foxes frequently cover about half a square mile in a night's foraging. They have a busy gait, always looking as if they are about to break from a fox-trot into a gallop, and swim and climb well. In mountains each fox's home range may cover 15 square miles (40 square kilometres); in residential suburbs their home ranges may be as small as 0.1 square mile (0.26 square kilometres).

In recent years so-called 'urban' foxes have created much interest. In Britain especially foxes seem to have taken to towns and cities. (Having said this they may be found in parts of Boston, New York, Montreal, Brisbane, Paris, Stockholm, Copenhagen, Essen and other cities.) Even in Britain however their numbers may vary from town to town because it is not so much urban areas that foxes like as suburban areas. If they are to have a label it should be 'suburban' foxes. It is perhaps better to think of them just as 'foxes'; those living in towns are exactly the same as those living in rural and remote areas, although their habits may differ. There are even vulpine commuters, foxes who live outside the town and only come in during the night to find food. Foxes live at their highest density in urban areas, and this affects their behaviour: the young foxes cannot move far when they leave their parents, and a higher proportion of them never leave home at all. They also eat different food from country foxes: in the suburbs they can enjoy gourmet dustbin offerings and in industrial areas they will tend to eat more rats and pigeons. Although the numbers of foxes are high in towns, their life expectancy is lower than in the country: eighteen months rather than a couple of years.

There are probably plenty of reasons for foxes' success in the suburbs. The main ones are plentiful and easily obtained food and shelter in and around outbuildings and sheds. These and more were provided by the expansion of semi-detached housing, with large gardens, on the outskirts of towns and cities in the 1920s and 1930s. No doubt the absence of stray dogs, farmers, gamekeepers and hunts helped as well.

At that time the fox population was recovering from a low point. (In fact numbers were so low in the early years of the century that hunts imported foxes to provide their 'sport'.) It is difficult to pinpoint why this should have been. Gamekeepers and others have been blamed because of the number of foxes they killed. Hunts never killed enough to make any difference, and in any case they helped to maintain sufficient animals here to enable their recovery to take place. Most attempts to wipe out fox populations fail, so it may be that factors other than human interference caused the reduction in numbers.

Whatever the reasons for the decline suburbia provided ideal conditions for foxes, and as middle class Britain prospered so did they. Thus southern and Midland towns have more foxes, generally speaking, than northern towns.

The development of low density housing was a particularly British phenomenon which also explains why foxes are relatively less successful and prominent in cities in other parts of the world. In addition there is far less competition for them here compared to, for example, North America. There they have to contend with, amongst others, racoons, coyotes, bobcats and even cougars for tickets to the garden party.

That foxes have been our companions throughout recorded history is beyond doubt. The association must work in the foxes' favour with more benefits being gained than costs being incurred. For every fox killed by a car, snare or hunt, there are probably several being fed by people, sheltering in our buildings or taking other opportunities provided by life in the city. We must remember that those opportunities may involve domestic animals – they will take pet rabbits and guinea pigs, poultry and ornamental waterfowl.

If they can avoid it foxes will not attack other carnivores. Healthy adult dogs and cats are safe from attack, in fact they are more likely to chase foxes off 'their' territory. A moment's thought on the result of most dog and cat encounters will serve to demonstrate that it is usually the cat that outfaces the dog, and so it will be with fox and cat encounters. Throughout nature similar sized predators tend to leave each other alone; picking on someone their own size is definitely not a good idea. Easy meals are what is wanted, not potentially fatal fights which take a lot of energy for little return. This means that foxes will take young, unhealthy and dead animals, and this gives rise to most of the stories of foxes eating some-one's moggie. Foxes may even play with domestic dogs in a most endearing fashion.

In January foxes are dispersing and mating. At this time the unearthly wails of vixens in the small hours startle many a late-night reveller or insomniac, and perhaps rival the honking of Canada geese in bringing the shades of wild lands to domestic suburbia. I have seen calling vixens sitting on car roofs, just as black-birds will perch high up to broadcast their songs. Both sexes can scream and bark, but generally it is the vixens that do the screaming and the dog foxes that do the barking.

If the serenading leads to successful mating the vixen will then find a suitable place for her breeding earth. 'Suitable' in this context seems to mean almost any-where reasonably warm and dry, frequently inside a building, whether or not it is occupied. Chosen sites are not always under floors – foxes have bred in roof spaces and in false ceilings. Offices, houses and schools have all provided nurser-ies for fox cubs. One school in Birmingham had to close some classrooms because of the overpowering smell from the fox earth beneath the floors. That fox family was persuaded to leave by putting speakers into the space they occupied and playing loud rock music to them.

Through October and November the family groups break up and young foxes disperse to try and establish their own territories. In December those that have done so break into song and start the whole process off again.

Foxes are many people's 'brush' with nature. For a wild carnivore they are fairly well behaved in human company, and bring pleasure to many people. (And perhaps vice-versa. An adult fox once leapt on to my lounge window sill and

watched the television for a few minutes. It may not have been impressed however because it did not return.) The fact they are still around shows how tough and resourceful they are. Most of the animals they shared this island with thousands of years ago are now long gone. Towns and cities, civilisations indeed, may come and go. Through it all it seems likely that Reynard will be there – on the one hand waving goodbye, and on the other waving to welcome a new lot of opportunities.

Racoons on the rampage

In North America one of the most successful urban colonisers has been the racoon, which tolerates much human activity as it sprawls in a tree during the day, and makes an unholy din at night as it rummages in dustbins. Urban racoons tend to be smaller than their rural cousins who live in colder woodlands. They also live at a much higher desnity of one every three acres rather than one every fifty acres. Though they are smaller, urban racoons generally live longer, provided they do not succumb to disease, which can be far more serious in the crowded town conditions. Humans both deliberately and unwittingly provide a feast for them and many relish the co-existence.

HEDGEHOGS

These spiny hunters and scavengers are ideally suited to suburban life. They have been around for about 15 million years – a lot longer than towns and cities – and would naturally forage along woodland edges and in grassy glades created by falling forest trees. To a hedgehog suburban gardens, churchyards and parks are just like those ancient glades. The worms, snails, slugs, beetles and caterpillars provide the same juicy dinners, the open but sheltered conditions are similar, and the leaves and grasses provide the same nesting material.

Hedgehogs do not depend upon humans or their activities, but are adaptable and general enough in their habits to be able to take advantage of them. They are, however, just as happy on a beach as in a garden. (Another link with the sea is their old name of 'urchin'. Because of their spines sea urchins were named after hedgehogs – today they should really be called 'sea hedgehogs'.)

Terrestrial hedgehogs are surprisingly active, being able to climb trees, walls and fences. They will roam about 1-2 miles (2-3 kilometres) a night, although about 1.5 miles is typical. A male (boar) will keep within an area of about 60 acres, whereas a female (sow) is content with about 20. The variety of feeding, breeding, resting and nesting places offered by suburbia means that they are here to stay.

Their adaptability is shown by their presence in the hearts of our major cities, although there are less there now than there were in mediaeval times. One famous example of a city centre hedgehog was found at the Ministry of Defence in Whitehall. Perhaps, like the security men, it was searching for moles.

Many people encourage hedgehogs to live in their gardens and put out food to attract them. This is quite all right (bread and milk is popular, although not ideal as the sole hedgehog diet, as it causes diarrhoea if fed exclusively; pet food or meat scraps are much better for them) and it is relatively easy to have your fast food franchise included on a hedgehog's night out. Animals soon learn where to go for easy meals and will return again and again. Some even learn to climb in through cat flaps. They do not only feed at night. After summer storms they often come out to dine during daylight, especially if the rain has enticed worms on to the lawn.

Putting out food only satisfies part of the hedgehog's needs. To really make them feel at home think of providing a five star hotel rather than a roadside café. This means making sure that your garden has places for nesting (both for breeding in the summer and for hibernation in the winter), plenty of natural food, and lots of cover. Hedgehogs are much happier beneath shrubs than in the middle of lawns. They want a few leaves, brushwood piles or compost heaps in undisturbed corners to curl up in, and they must have a balanced diet to remain healthy. If your garden provides these things then hedgehogs may make themselves at home even without extra feeding. (I know of a female who chose a black plastic bag filled with garden waste to bring up her young, to the chagrin of the gardener who then had to leave the bag *in situ* for longer than intended.)

Hedgehogs have a curious habit of anointing their spines with saliva

Gardens may provide tasty meals and comfortable quarters for hedgehogs, but they also present a lot of dangers. Slug pellets can result in poisoned snacks, ponds with smooth sides can become watery graves and strimmers can slice through sleeping hedgehogs hidden in leaves or long grass. All of these things can be avoided: let the hedgehogs deal with the slugs, make sure there is an escape route from your ponds (chicken wire dangled in the water will suffice) and check for slumberers in the shrubbery before starting work. Perhaps the greatest danger for garden hedgehogs is the autumn bonfire. Piles of sticks and leaves make apparently good nesting and hibernation places. Before starting fires check to make sure that there are no sleepy residents.

Although their spiny coats give protection from predators, and provide landing cushions for unintentional hedgehog aviators, they may have disadvantages. They are said to be very difficult to groom. One animal's problem is always another animal's opportunity, and so it is that hedgehogs are often infested with large numbers of fleas and ticks. This view is not universally accepted, some people think that hedgehogs are just lazy groomers. Certainly their curious habit of anointing their spines with frothy saliva demonstrates that they are not averse to pushing their sensitive noses into their own spines.

With very few natural enemies (some animals like foxes and badgers can learn to unroll them) and plenty of food and cover in towns and cities this appears to be one animal that has adapted to people without changing its own lifestyle. It may be that there is a greater density of hedgehogs in our suburbs than in nearby countryside. They are also found in inner suburbs and in the central London parks. One reason for this may be the slightly higher temperatures, with extra frost-free days which must help second-brood youngsters by giving them a little more time to build up their fat reserves for hibernation. This may be balanced by the fact that although hedgehogs truly hibernate (as compared to squirrels which merely rest during the coldest spells, and being seed eaters can lay in winter stores) they are restless hibernators and will awake on mild days. This uses up their reserves and reduces their chances of surviving the winter. The danger is illustrated by their heartbeat – 120 times a minute when active and 55 times a minute, or less, when hibernating.

The dangers and delights of urban life must cancel themselves out overall as the hedgehog population never seems to change very much. A little help from their friends is always welcome, but mind you do not run over your spiny guests while fetching the pet food for them from the supermarket.

GREY SQUIRRELS

To some, grey squirrels are the epitome of urban wildlife – lively, sharp and cheeky. To others they are a menace and a health hazard – nothing but rats with bushy tails.

They are probably seen more often by more people than any other wild mammal in Britain. This is not due to particularly high numbers – other rodents such as mice and rats are more numerous – but rather to their lifestyle. Grey squirrels are active in the day above ground, and are not at all shy of people, or the places people live. In fact given a loose soffit board, and a handy branch, wire or pipe, and squirrels will move happily into buildings.

This unwarranted familiarity is all the more surprising because until just over 150 years ago grey squirrels were unknown on this side of the Atlantic. Even today their presence in Europe is almost entirely confined to the British Isles.

The British love-hate relationship with grey squirrels started in the middle of the 19th century. In about 1830 they were reported from Denbighshire and Montgomeryshire, but the origins of those animals are unknown. In 1876 a Cheshire landowner released animals brought from America. Other people soon followed suit and many populations became established throughout the British Isles. For about fifty years these caused little concern or comment. Writing in 1921 Edward Step was able to treat London's grey squirrel population as something of a curiosity, remarking that the Regent's Park animals originated from over-populated cages in London Zoo. This group expanded into the suburbs and he expected that 'British naturalists of a not-too-distant future will probably have to include two species of squirrels in their lists.' (Entomologists might add that they brought with them a flea specific to grey squirrels, which is now also established in this country.)

Some idea of grey squirrels' powers of rapid colonisation can be gleaned from the fact that the progeny of a pair of squirrels released at Finnart in Scotland in 1892 had spread over an area of 300 square miles by 1915. This ability to breed quickly and to disperse over large areas, together with the availability of an empty 'niche' (greys prefer deciduous to conifer woodlands, reds' preference is the other way round) meant that isolated populations soon linked up.

All attempts to eliminate them have failed. A hundred squirrels a year were shot at Kew Gardens from 1917 to 1937 with no appreciable effects on the local population. Nationally, between 1953 and 1955, free cartridges were given out, and a bounty of a shilling a squirrel was paid. After the bounty was doubled and more than £100,000 had been paid out, the scheme was abandoned in 1958 – and the squirrels were still with us.

Despite these great successes (from the squirrels' point of view) it is curious that there were none in Buckingham Palace Gardens as late as the 1960s. The managers of the royal parks tried to eliminate squirrels for many years, but why they should have succeeded here when they failed elsewhere is something of a mystery. In the end though the squirrels won – by the early '80s they were having their own royal garden party. Unlike the other palace residents nobody put the flags out to show they were in residence.

Squirrels may cause severe damage to trees, especially hardwood trees. This is generally caused in three ways. They eat shoots and seeds, they use young shoots and green leaves to build their dreys, and they strip bark from trunks to get at the soft and nutritious inner bark. The latter is often the most serious problem because the squirrels tend to nibble away the bark all around the trunk, causing the tree to die above the bark ring. Fairly young trees between 20 and 40 years old, especially sycamore, beech, oak, ash and birch, are their favourites for this treatment.

Having said this grey squirrels will eat almost anything – fruit, fungi, carrion, young birds and eggs, crops, bulbs, fish and honey. This catholic taste in food helps to explain their success, especially in towns and cities where people provide a permanent buffet of squirrel takeaways. In Shepherds Bush Green, London, feeding boxes are provided for the squirrels and people are encouraged to keep them stocked with food. Such easy living may also explain why, despite the abundance of squirrels and their potential to damage trees, such damage is rarely reported from parks and gardens. The extra food found in towns may be an important factor, especially in the summer. The period between the emergence of spring shoots and the availability of autumn fruits and nuts is a difficult one, and is when squirrels are most likely to nibble bark. On the other hand serious damage did occur in Lafayette Park, over the road from the White House in Washington. The squirrels were eating annual plants and damaging mature trees, causing an estimated $4,500 damage every year. This was blamed on the large numbers of squirrels in the park, which in turn was a result of feeding by the public. If you do feed your local squirrels close encounters are not recommended, their claws are sharp enough to be painful if they climb over you, and they can inflict painful bites.

Squirrels climb buildings as easily as trees

Although they damage trees, squirrels also help them to grow. In the autumn they collect acorns, beech mast, chestnuts and other fruits, and bury them. They usually only bury one item at a time, although there are frequent reports of caches of nuts and fruits being found in buildings. They dig up their buried treasures during the winter, such activity being most noticeable when snow is on the ground. As many squirrels do not survive the winter, and assuming that they do not in any case remember where they have left every acorn, many trees must now be growing as a result of squirrel hoarding.

Grey squirrels are of course noted for their agility and alertness. It helps to sell beer, but more importantly it helps them to escape from danger. They have very good eyesight and a good sense of smell. They spend a lot of time foraging on the ground and need to be ready to spring back into the safety of the trees. They can run up and down tree trunks, swing paw over paw beneath branches, wires and lines, and use their tails both for balance and to hang down to reach juicy morsels.

Trees may be their natural habitat but squirrels will readily take to life indoors. Wildlife agencies receive a constant stream of enquiries about what to do with the squirrels in the loft. That they should be evicted is certain – their adventurous taste in foods can lead to them sampling the insulation on electric cables. Achieving this is more difficult. Once they are outside the solution is to block up the place where they are getting in, having checked first to make sure there is not a nestful of youngsters inside.

Our parks and gardens are now permanent homes for grey squirrels. We have to come to terms with this, controlling them where necessary, not overfeeding them, but otherwise enjoying their antics. If the worst comes to the worst we could perhaps revive some old recipes from America where at one time grey squirrels were hunted for the pot – it being said that 'either fried or in a stew, (they) are a tasty treat'.

RATS AND MICE

Young couples may dream of the pitter patter of tiny feet, but the dream may become a nightmare if the tiny feet belong to rats or mice. As their name suggests, house mice are more likely to be found in houses, rats preferring larger buildings, such as warehouses, or the hidden world of sewers, ducts and tunnels. Both species may be joined by close relatives in their chosen abodes: house mice by field mice, and brown rats by black rats. Together with feral pigeons and cockroaches, house mice and brown rats can thrive in the heart of the largest and dirtiest cities.

Neither house mice or brown and black rats are native to Britain, or even to Europe. House mice originated in Asia near what is now the Russian Turkestan / Iranian border. They may have been the first mammals to be brought here by people, probably arriving during the Iron Age. (Goats and voles were introduced at about the same time.) Rats arrived much more recently from their wild haunts south of the Himalayas. As recently as the 13th century black rats had only spread to the Middle East, but they then hitched lifts with returning crusaders. Within a couple of hundred years they had established large populations all over western Europe, brought the catastrophe of the Black Death (bubonic plague, carried by their fleas) and provided employment to apothecaries (who supplied rat poisons) and rat-catchers. They made enough impact to give rise to the tale of the Pied Piper of Hamelin (said to have performed his work in 1284) and to be mentioned

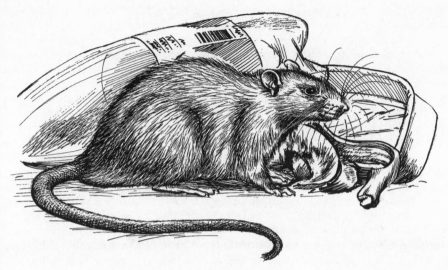

Rats eat almost anything

in the works of Chaucer and Langland in the late 1300s. In 1469 the accounts of St Michael's Church in Cornhill included an item for buying rat traps.

Black rats prospered for 500 years, newcomers continually arriving in ships. In the 18th century, however, those same ships provided transport for their cousin the brown rat. This now familiar species displaced the black rats to the extent that today black rats are one of Europe's rarest mammals, surviving only in ports, where until recent years ships still carried rat stowaways, and one or two other places. In the 1940s black rats were still more common than brown rats in the City of London and around Oxford St. They were non-fee-paying members of some of the smartest clubs, and had free access to the shows at many theatres and cinemas. Now it seems that after a mere 700 years their time with us is coming to an end.

The black rat's lifestyle puts it at a disadvantage compared to its brown cousin. It originally lived in trees and still likes to climb. It makes its home in roof and loft spaces and is much easier to catch and kill than the brown rat. The latter lives mainly underground, concealing itself from its human enemies. In addition brown rats will outcompete black rats where they occur together. In 1768 a rat catcher observed that after putting both species in one cage the brown rats killed all the black rats.

Brown rats are such a recent arrival that their spread through Europe is precisely documented. They arrived in south-east Europe in the middle of the 16th century, and in 1727 large numbers are said to have crossed the Volga river following an earthquake. They then spread throughout the continent, slowly by land but more quickly by ship. They arrived in England in 1728 or 1729. Like a lot of pests they then acquired a nickname associated with an unpopular group of people – in this case they were called Hanoverian rats. The new Protestant monarchy stood accused of importing them on the ships that brought William of Orange, and, later, George I, to these shores. People who thought they knew more about natural history than politics suggested that they had really arrived from Norway, hence their scientific name of *Rattus norvegicus*. These people were wrong as well because they did not get to Norway for another 35 years.

Landlocked Switzerland escaped them until 1809, and even Paris was free of rats until 1750. We took them to America in 1775, and they were in Vancouver by 1887. Considering what a pest they are it is amazing that we were so careless as to spread these animals throughout the northern hemisphere in just over 150 years!

Brown rats are now abundant in our city centres. Thousands of them live beneath our feet in sewers and other underground tunnels. If there are not enough man-made tunnels they will dig their own beneath floors and paving. It is likely that wherever you are at ground level in a British city there is at least one rat within 50 metres of you at all times! They will eat anything, can breed all year round, are rightly suspicious of people and seem to be here to stay. There are enormous numbers of them. In 1943-44 650,000 were killed in London's sewers during a campaign to protect wartime food supplies.

House mice are much smaller cousins to rats. Conveniently for both species they have different habits. Where brown rats prefer to live around rather than in buildings, urban house mice are happy indoors. These mice are 'commensal' with humans, a word literally meaning 'sharing the same table' but which is applied to any species which depends upon living in close association with another.

House mice have mimicked their human hosts by spreading throughout the world from one relatively small area (in our case East Africa, in theirs the steppes of Russian Turkestan) and by developing into a number of distinct races. Each race of mouse is ideally suited to the places where it is found – some still living wild, some close to, but not wholly dependant upon people, and some living entirely in our buildings. Even in a country as small as Britain these differences have been observed, with separate populations living in buildings, on and around farms, and in the countryside. It is not just a question of circumstances affecting behaviour. In 1905 house mice were living in every house on the island of St Kilda. The last 36 people living there left on August 28th, 1930 – by 1938 the house mice had died out; without people they could not sustain themselves. Where there are people though they can thrive in the most unlikely places, such as coal mines and frozen meat stores. In the meat stores they subsist on meat alone, in total darkness and in temperatures of -10°Centigrade.

Surviving in the dark is not too much of a problem for house mice, which are mainly nocturnal creatures. Although they have perfectly good eyesight (but they are probably colour blind) their most highly developed sense is their sense of

Mice are often seen on underground stations

smell. The three blind mice of the nursery rhyme were not really the disadvantaged rodents we have been led to believe. A group of mice, usually an extended family with a dominant male, his harem of females and several generations of their offspring, will know every scent in their territory. Indeed they will be responsible for most of them, as they mark objects and places like the edges of shelves with urine. The scents left not only help to identify objects in their dark landscape, but also identify the individual mouse, its status, its sex and its breeding condition. Having the usual rodent's need to keep its sharp teeth honed, life for a house mouse has been said to be all nibble and dribble.

Signposts and dental health for mice mean disease and damage for their human landlords. The constant battle between mice and men has been going on for many centuries. It is perhaps surprising that the first known mention of a mousetrap is as late as about 1450, and, yes, cheese was the bait! Since then a great deal of ingenuity and not a little cruelty has gone into making better mousetraps. But the mice seem to be able to outwit them all. Five hundred years on, in 1945, Richard Fitter said that 'Few houses in London can boast of being entirely free from house mice scampering along the wainscoting.' Modern technology may, however, have finally cracked the problem. Pest control companies now have an electronic trap which not only holds the mouse until it can be despatched, but calls the person who has to do the despatching and triggers a computer to print a report detailing the whole affair. This seems very efficient, but there have been super mice who specialise in gnawing through computer cables ...

In the 1960s and 1970s increases in mouse populations were reported, but today there seem to be fewer about. In the mid 1980s Mike Birkhead and Gavin Weightman thought that they were 'probably less common' in London, but could still be 'found everywhere, and they are often seen on underground stations'.

Warfare is sometimes suspended. Ancient Greeks and Romans worshipped mice, and as recently as the 16th century this practice persisted. In Britain eating mice was claimed to be a cure for coughs and throat infections.

Presumably cats were not too popular at mouse worshipping ceremonies, although their reputation as mouse catchers is very inflated. They have dined out, or rather in, for years on the belief that they control mice. Ecological theory is against this belief (predator numbers are controlled by prey numbers, not the other way round) and apart from this a bowl of choice pet food every day ensures that most of them do not have any reason for chasing the tiny mice. In any case the mice can easily escape through holes that even thin, let alone fat, cats cannot get through.

House mice can vary their breeding rate to suit local conditions. In theory one female can have up to 70 young in 13 or 14 litters a year, but in practice they will have between 30 and 50. Mice living on farms used to reach enormous numbers inside cosy hayricks as they bred as fast as possible. In buildings they tend to breed in smaller numbers averaging about 5.5 litters a year, each with an average of 5.5 young.

Houses, especially those close to suitable open spaces, are frequently invaded by field mice. These are altogether smarter mice than their urban brethren, with sleek brown coats and big appealing eyes. They are just as obnoxious in their habits though and should not be encouraged. In my house they have spoilt food left in the cooker overnight, nibbled every apple and pear in the fruit bowl, and dug great holes in the soil of plant pots. The last activity is characteristic in that they only go one way, and so there is a big hole down one side of the plant, and an equally big one on the other side where they have come out again. Modern burglar alarms can be sensitive to the movements of mice of either variety and may be set off by their nocturnal perambulations. This is just the latest way in which these impudent lodgers torment us. They will no doubt remain one jump (or scurry) ahead of humans – perhaps we should change the epithet 'Mickey Mouse operation' from an insult to a compliment.

WATER VOLES

Despite the fact that water voles are found throughout Britain, most people are unaware of them. This apparent contradiction is typical of this loveable rodent. Whilst real water voles go unnoticed the character 'Ratty' in *The Wind in the Willows* is known to every generation of children. Partly because of author Kenneth Graham's unfortunate and misleading choice of name, water voles are often taken for rats, and persecuted rather than tolerated. They thrive in the artificial environment of our canal system and yet are in serious decline. In this country water voles are rarely found far from water, but on the European mainland they can be a serious pest of cereal crops. Perhaps we should put the record straight, at least in relation to British water voles, by applying Ratty's own words – about Toad – to himself: 'He is indeed the best of animals, so simple, so good-natured ... he has some great qualities.'

Water voles spend their lives in and around slow-flowing waterways or ponds and lakes. They seem to ignore people and tolerate poor quality water. I can remember seeing a water vole sitting in the middle of a small river chewing grass stems while dozens of people passed within a few feet. Canals might have been designed with voles in mind, especially where they have plants and banks along their edges. This is one reason why water voles are often found in the heart of urban areas, despite their national decline.

Water is used to escape from danger and because of this they are more often heard than seen. When alarmed a water vole will drop into water with a distinctive 'plop'. Its presence and progress may then be revealed by a line of bubbles moving quickly away from the bank. Sometimes a vole will kick up a cloud of silt to confuse its pursuer. On other occasions the animal will pop its head out of the water and search for the cause of its alarm from a safe distance, looking on these occasions like a tiny seal.

Although waterways and their surroundings are the natural habitat for water voles they are basically land animals which use water for security. (Their scientific name, *Arvicola terrestris*, emphasises this.) They cannot stay in water for very long as their fur becomes waterlogged, and they do not generally feed in water but on bankside plants. They will eat snails and dead fish but do not try to catch fish. They dig burrows in banks with entrances above and below water. When they escape into the water it is to find one of their underwater burrow entrances. Many of their burrows' passages and nests are connected, but some are just isolated bolt-holes.

There should never be any confusion with rats. Compared with rats, water voles have rounded not pointed muzzles, almost invisible not prominent ears, a shorter and hairy tail (about 60% of the length of the head and body) rather than a longer and naked one (at least 80% of the length of the head and body) and usually reddish rather than brownish fur. (Some water vole populations in northern Scotland and East Anglia are black, and black or partly white individuals can occur anywhere.)

'He is indeed the best of animals...'

Voles do not live very long. One reason for this is their place on the menu of many other creatures. Their main enemies are stoats and mink. Other predators include herons, barn owls, rats, pike and, especially in urban areas, dogs and cats.

Despite the dogs and cats, urban areas may be the water voles' salvation. Recent studies have shown that they have disappeared from nearly 70% of the places they were living at the turn of the century. Their decline started before mink arrived to make things worse. The presence in towns of many stretches of water suitable for water voles, together with their tolerance of both humans and poor water quality, may help to conserve this harmless and attractive animal. They are found for example in flooded gravel pits in the Lea Valley in London, in the canals of the West Midlands, and in the industrial north-west in the Trent and Mersey, Leeds and Liverpool and St Helen's canals. The studies also show that after marshland and grassland they are most likely to be found in suburban and urban areas.

Urban rivers are less likely to be of help because they tend to be more polluted than even water voles can tolerate, and their water levels rise and fall very rapidly. The sudden changes in water level can wash away banks with burrows in them, expose underwater burrow entrances and scour bankside vegetation which the voles need for food. It is not beyond possibility that large garden ponds, if they have suitable banks, will attract water voles to breed, although it is more likely that wandering individuals will turn up in gardens close to existing breeding sites.

SNAKES AND LIZARDS

There are only three species of snake – adder, grass snake and smooth snake – and three species of lizard – common lizard, sand lizard and slow-worm – native to this country. All of them may be encountered in urban, or at least suburban areas, but only grass snakes, slow-worms and common lizards are likely to thrive in them. The lifestyles of the others do not fit them for the bright lights. Adders and sand lizards for example are often found on heathlands. When these are overtaken by expanding urban areas the animals may become unwilling citizens until their colonies die out. This was the fate of the smooth snake in the 19th century. It was first recognised as a British species from a snake captured in Bournemouth in 1859. Subsequently it was found to be very common in that part of Dorset. As Bournemouth grew from a small village to the bustling resort it is today so the snakes declined.

Sand lizards – one of the 21 species in English Nature's Species Recovery Programme – are also found in the Bournemouth and Poole area, as well as Merseyside, Hampshire and Surrey. (English Nature's Species Recovery Programme has been devised to increase the populations and ranges of a number of declining or threatened species of plants and animals in the United Kingdom. A plan of action for each of the species has been drawn up and is now being implemented with the help of conservation agencies such as the wildlife trusts.) In Brighton in 1994 a colony of more than 100 slow-worms was rescued when their habitat was lost to a new development. Brighton Urban Wildlife Group were able to catch these legless lizards because of their preference for basking underneath debris such as corrugated iron, and move them to a safe new home.

Work in London in the early 1990s showed that grass snakes, adders, slow-worms and common lizards were to be found within a 20-mile radius of St Paul's Cathedral – the traditional definition of the City for natural historians. Having said this, numbers of grass snakes and common lizards were found to be declining, adders were only found in two places, and it was thought they would soon be extinct in the capital. Common lizards and slow-worms were abundant in a few places but were missing from large areas. Of the four the slow-worm produced the most records. The same four species were discovered in Oxford in the 1980s.

In other parts of the world where reptiles are more numerous gardening can become an exciting pastime. In Australia blue-tongued lizards and pythons lurk in the shrubberies. In the eastern United States the black rat snake often does a passable impression of the garden hose, or suddenly appears overhead as it slithers out of a tree. In mainland Europe lizards and snakes are much more frequently encountered than in Britain, wall lizards being often seen.

Grass snakes are the most common of our three snakes. They grow to about five feet, like plenty of cover, such as rough grassland, and to be near to water. They are greenish-brown, with black spots along the sides and tops of their bodies, and a distinct collar, or ring, just behind their heads. They will take readily to canals and ponds, enjoying nothing more than a tasty frog or two for supper. When alarmed, a grass snake may feign death, rolling over and lying with its tongue lolling out of its mouth. The London survey showed that they favour open, undisturbed places near to the river, sewage works, old gravel pits and golf courses. They are mainly found in the north and east of the city.

Grass snakes are at their north-western limit in the British Isles. Like all reptiles they are cold blooded, which means that they need warm sunshine to survive. They are not found in Scotland, although the slow-worm, common lizard and adder, which all bear live young, are. Grass snakes do occur in Scandinavia, 700 miles further north than Scotland, but this is because the temperature there in July is similar to that in the English Midlands, and the snakes can survive the harsher winter in good hibernation sites. Urban areas help the snakes because they tend to be warmer, although this benefit is offset by their aversion to people – if there is one thing stronger than people's dislike of snakes it is snakes' dislike of people. What does suit them, however, are the large number of pools and canals in towns, and the many garden compost heaps. In 1993 there was an unusually high number of grass snakes reported from gardens, but it is not known why.

The interior of compost heaps is warmer than the outside, and grass snakes will seek them out to lay their eggs. The heaps are perfect incubators which help the embryos in the eggs to develop fast enough to survive their first winter. After cool summers many young snakes that do not have this warmer welcome to the world die. Because snakes do not like people this behaviour of seeking out artificial nursery sites is unusual, and is shared by only one other species in Europe. As well as compost heaps grass snakes have been known to lay their eggs in manure heaps, hayricks, piles of sawdust and holes in the walls of bakeries.

Grass snakes feed on any small animals that are available. Their liking for water, sometimes swimming with the head held vertically, like miniature Loch Ness monsters, means that frogs, newts, fish and tadpoles are frequently taken. Small birds and mammals are also eaten if they can be caught. Young snakes are themselves the frequent victims of passing predators, being much like big and juicy worms. A hazard for larger snakes in gardens is netting. They can become entangled and die, because they can slither the front of their body into the mesh, but their backward facing scales stop them slithering out again.

Compost heaps make good incubators for grass snakes' eggs

Like many other creatures with the word 'common' in their name common lizards should be renamed because they are now uncommon. Most people will go through life without ever seeing a lizard or being aware of their presence. For example, for years hundreds of thousands of commuters going in and out of Paddington Station rattled their way past a large colony of hundreds of lizards near to Wormwood Scrubs. When engineering work on the new Channel Tunnel links started in 1989 the lizards' home was faced with destruction. A rescue was organised which involved taking many of the lizards into care before releasing them at two specially prepared sites nearby. The commuters still rattle their way in and out of the city, the lizards are enjoying their new abode, and they are both blissfully unaware of each other.

This species also lives on some of the islands in the River Thames. The key to their success on the islands and alongside the railway lines is the lack of disturbance. These are places visited by few people. The island populations are also helped by the absence of cats, which are as lethal to lizards as they are to other small creatures.

The heat radiated from the bricks and mortar of our towns ought to suit lizards very well, but even the wall lizard has difficulty surviving here. Two hundred were released in Paignton in 1937, and there were still some there in the 1960s, but the colony declined rather than expanded. The species does live in Jersey, and one colony has survived for many years on the Isle of Wight.

Because reptiles are often kept as pets, escaped or abandoned individuals are frequently found. Terrapins are amongst the most commonly encountered exotics. They often survive for years in warm pools, but they are unable to breed successfully in the wild in Britain. Fortunately we do not have alligators in our sewers and waterways as do some American cities. Neither do we have to worry about their cousins the crocodiles, unlike people in some of Africa's growing cities.

AMPHIBIANS

Amphibians are declining all over the world. The causes are uncertain, but may be related to atmospheric pollution. They are very sensitive to this as many of them breathe through their skins as well as their lungs. It is ironic therefore that this is one group that we really seem to be helping in our polluted towns and cities. The current fashion for garden ponds is providing four of our six native species with new habitat to compensate for the loss of thousands of ponds in rural areas. In addition canals, ornamental ponds in parks, relic farm ponds now surrounded by suburbia, and a host of temporary water bodies can accommodate small populations of frogs, toads or newts.

I know of newts that have bred for years in a discarded metal water tank in a garden, and in the few inches of water lying in the water jump of a school athletics track. The conservation value of garden ponds should not be underestimated because over the country as a whole common frogs and common toads are not really common any more. The ponds particularly suit frogs and smooth newts, but toads and great crested newts benefit from them as well. Our help is repaid with interest because all amphibians relish the slugs, snails and insects which cause so much anguish to gardeners.

Another factor helping frogs and toads is that many people welcome, or at least tolerate them in their gardens: they have become 'fashionable'. Toads in particular used to be thought of with revulsion, but now they are generally well regarded, and even have their own road signs. Perhaps the fairy stories about their being princes and princesses in disguise have helped their image!

The six species of amphibians native to this country are the common frog, common and natterjack toads, and smooth, palmate and great-crested newts. There is some evidence that a seventh species, the pond frog, is also native, but this has not yet been accepted. They all need water for breeding, places to hibernate and plenty of cover for feeding and safety. All except the natterjack toad and the palmate newt are frequently found in gardens that are not over tidy, and in sheltered spots in parks and informally managed or neglected open spaces.

Many books say that amphibians and fish do not mix, and that goldfish and other ornamental fish will prevent amphibians from breeding. This is not true. Fish will make a meal of tadpoles and young amphibians, but frogs and toads will spawn year after year in ponds containing goldfish, the number of tadpoles they produce being sufficient for some of them to survive. Newts have more trouble succeeding permanently alongside fish, and for this reason they do better in ponds that dry up from time to time. As amphibians breed for some years they can survive a season with no offspring. Fish, however, cannot manage without permanent water and do not survive the drying out of ponds.

Tadpoles are so called as a result of two old words being combined – 'tade' or 'tadde', the old name for toads, and 'poll' meaning head. Frog tadpoles hatch from masses of spawn, toad tadpoles from strings of spawn and newt tadpoles

Frogs are smoother than toads (RIGHT) Mating time for frogs is late winter

from single eggs wrapped in the leaves of underwater plants. Most of them feed for a few months in the summer before changing into miniature adults. A few tadpoles never make this change, but continue to grow into giant tadpoles. This is called neoteny, and is widespread amongst amphibians worldwide. Some species can breed in this state. Neotenous frog tadpoles may grow to 12 centimetres (4.7 in.).

Smooth newts, and the protected great-crested newts, are not seen as often as frogs and toads. This is because they spend much less time at the surface of their chosen ponds, and they are more active by night than by day. The best way to see them is to take a torch out after dark and shine it in the shallows of ponds. The names 'smooth' and 'great crested' serve only to confuse when trying to identify these two species. Female great-crested newts do not have a crest, and male smooth newts do! Variations in colour and size increase the confusion. Males are the easiest to tell apart as the male smooth newt has an unbroken crest from head to tail, whereas the male great-crested newt has a marked notch in his at the base of the tail, as well as a distinctive silvery stripe along the side of the tail.

Like frogs and toads, both species enter ponds in late winter to lay their eggs. Tadpoles hatch after about four weeks, and can be told from frog and toad tad-

poles by their feathery external gills. Adults and most young newts leave the water in mid to late summer and take refuge in the surrounding vegetation. Most animals stay within a few hundred metres of their home pond but youngsters wander further away than adults, and may not return to breed for three years. From October or November to February or March newts hibernate on land before returning to the pond that spawned them to start the breeding cycle again. They are rarely seen during the day unless disturbed in their hiding places beneath stones and logs. They can turn up inside buildings, especially cellars and undisturbed outhouses. Dozens of great-crested newts were found living in fine style in the cellars of a Victorian hall alongside an ornamental lake, about five miles from Birmingham City centre.

Great-crested newts enjoy protection under both British and European laws. Neither the newts, their tadpoles or their breeding ponds should be disturbed without a licence. This is because over the last fifty years their numbers have crashed as ponds have been destroyed. Luckily they are still numerous in some places and a lot of these 'newt hot-spots' are in towns and cities. For example in the Black Country towns of the West Midlands there are many ponds where they still breed.

Frogs are much more lively, more numerous, more noisy and spend more time in the water than newts or toads. They will frequently be seen hopping in and out of their breeding ponds, or lurking like miniature crocodiles with just the top half of their heads above water, watching your every move. One thing to be thankful for in Britain is that their croak is subdued, sounding rather like a distant motorbike. In some countries the frogs' chorus is loud and unceasing. Suburbanites in the eastern United States have to put up with a real racket from species such as tree frog and spring peeper.

When frogs and toads do leave the water they need protection from the local birds, and plenty of long grass and shrubs is ideal for them. Such an area will also be rich in the insects, slugs and snails which are their favourite foods. As well as some gardens, informal parts of parks and the typical tall vegetation alongside many canals suits them very well. It is this combination of small water bodies set in informally or lightly managed open spaces and gardens that is the secret of their new-found success in towns.

When winter comes male frogs return to their breeding ponds or canals and hibernate in the mud at the bottom. (Some ponds seem to have frogs in and around them the whole time, presumably these are males who just do not stray away in mid summer.) Female and young frogs hibernate on land, beneath stones, logs or leaves. They do not indulge in mass returns in the spring in the way that toads do, but seem to slip back to the water unnoticed, except presumably by the waiting males. Problems can arise when ponds have been destroyed since the frogs left. If houses are built on the site then the following spring new owners can find themselves playing host to lots of frustrated frogs. Occasional tales of 'plagues of frogs' probably result from this situation, although I cannot vouch for the biblical version.

Large numbers of toads making their annual pilgrimage to their breeding ponds often cause a stir as well. Their determination to return to 'their' pond, regardless of man-made inconveniences such as roads, often results in large numbers being killed. Many people now act as lollipop persons for these amorous toads. Fluorescent jackets, torches and buckets are pressed into action as the shuffling toads make their slow but steady way to their watery nuptial beds. Highway authorities now erect warning signs at more than 400 recognised crossing points throughout the country.

The amphibians are one of the smallest groups of animals in this country but four out of the six of them seem to be able to exploit modern urban conditions – a greater proportion than in any other group. They are completely harmless to human interests and seem to provide endless fascination for people of all ages. There is no apparent reason why they should not continue to thrive, if not in the hearts of our cities, in the surrounding areas of suburbia.

BLACK REDSTARTS

Of all the truly wild animals and birds found in urban areas in this country black redstarts are probably the ones most exclusively tied to city centres. They almost always build their nests in large empty buildings close to open areas, with few or no trees and bushes. These somewhat exacting requirements just happened to be available in cities devastated by wartime bombing and then redeveloped bit by bit. Since then, the black redstarts have benefited from the redevelopment cycle of build, use, vacate, demolish and build again.

Black redstarts are members of a group of small thrush-like songbirds which includes robins, nightingales, wheatears and chats. They are generally a dull brownish grey, except for the bright chestnut tail, and the black throat and breast and white wing bars of adult males. Common redstarts are generally brighter, with more brown and red plumage. (Their name is derived from the Old English word 'steort' which meant 'tail'.) They eat insects, which they will take either on the ground or, flycatcher-like, on the wing.

The first few breeding pairs of modern times arrived here just before the Second World War. (Breeding was recorded in Durham in 1845.) In 1926 a pair bred at the Palace of Engineering in Wembley, and others bred occasionally through the 1930s. In 1927 a pair was frequently seen around the Natural History Museum in South Kensington, obviously seeking fame by going direct to the experts. Numbers slowly built up so that by 1942 there were 20 singing males in London, and birds were turning up in other parts of the country as well. In 1943 and 1944 they were in Birmingham, Coventry, Southampton and Rochester. In 1951 they were reported as being the only songsters in the City of London. They have continued to breed in small numbers since then.

Black redstarts build their nests in large empty buildings close to open areas with few trees or bushes

The limited success and behaviour of black redstarts in Britain is something of a mystery. Their arrival here may be explained by the fact that they have been expanding their range north and west across Europe for more than a hundred years. (The effect of the British Isles being at the edge of their range is demonstrated by the presence of birds at three different stages of their annual cycle – breeding pairs visiting for the summer, winter visitors, often on the south-west coast, who return to other countries to breed, and resident birds.)

More difficult to explain is their fondness for city centres and their apparent rejection of breeding habitat which they occupy on mainland Europe. As cliff- and hole-nesting birds they would be expected to favour buildings in general, but why they only use large empty ones is not clear. They seem to shun human disturbance here, but in other countries they are common around houses and gardens, and in villages and farmyards. They will nest in large buildings on the Continent, and many fine Gothic cathedrals act as giant nest boxes to black redstarts. Some of the first birds in London were seen around Westminster Abbey.

It has been suggested that there are still too few birds in the United Kingdom to force them to compete with other species, such as robins, for anything other than ideal breeding territories. This implies that the garden dwelling black redstarts of France and Holland are in what the experts call 'sub-optimal' habitats (less than perfect places). We will have to wait and see if our population of this species builds up sufficiently to force them into closer contact with other species and with people.

The West Midlands Bird Club has carried out intensive studies of the birds breeding in Birmingham. They have discovered that some youngsters return to the places they were born to breed themselves, but they have not been able to find out where these birds spend the winter. They have also found out that the extensive canal system in the West Midlands is used by black redstarts on migration. Before mating the males defend a territory of about 15 acres (6 hectares). An important finding related to this is that breeding males stop singing whilst their broods are in the nest, a period of about sixteen days, whereas lone male birds sing continuously through the summer. This fact is helping with estimates of breeding pairs as opposed to single birds holding territory but failing to attract mates. Birmingham's new International Convention Centre has taken one known breeding territory away, but birds are appearing just to the north. This is most appropriate – their red tails flash like jewels, and one area they are moving into is Birmingham's Jewellery Quarter.

It is possible for one pair of birds to raise three broods in a summer – the champion breeders are a pair which fledged ten young in one year. Such fecundity should enable the species to expand and to become more familiar to many people. Despite the presence of at least a few birds in the hearts of cities like Birmingham and London for over fifty years, most people remain completely unaware of them.

GULLS

Some birds, water rails for example, lead quiet unobtrusive lives, doing everything they can to remain unnoticed. Others, like warblers, make themselves prominent only when looking for a mate or holding territory. Gulls have no such inhibitions, they go around in gangs and are noisy, conspicuous and aggressive – typical perhaps of some townsfolk. It should come as no surprise therefore that they are taking to life in towns and cities, and that the name 'seagull' is becoming more and more inappropriate. Towns provide them with all they need – plenty of water (they do not seem to notice the difference between salt and fresh water), plenty of food (especially on rubbish dumps) and lots of imitation cliffs or open land to nest on. (Not all gulls are cliff nesters, black-headed, lesser black-backed and common gulls prefer to nest on the ground, herring gulls and kittiwakes will nest either on the ground or on cliffs and buildings.)

Having colonised coastal and estuary towns, gulls are now moving further and further inland. Unlike most birds and animals found in urban areas, gulls really are moving in. Their habitat has not been absorbed into towns, they have not been living with people for thousands of years, they have never been domesticated, and they have not even been living inland for very long. But slowly and surely their numbers are increasing.

In 1976 a study indicated that there were over 3,000 pairs of herring gulls nesting in urban areas and they were increasing by 17% a year. This was consistent with an increase in numbers of this species throughout Europe. Interestingly the urban gulls had better breeding success than those at their traditional nesting sites.

There are 45 species of gulls in the world, and a dozen of these may be spotted in London. Half a dozen of them are frequent or common both in London and other cities – greater and lesser black-backed, herring, black-headed and common gulls and kittiwakes. Many of them move inland in the winter, but more and more are now staying to breed. For years kittiwakes have bred on window sills on tall buildings in the north-east, and were known from Sheffield, Huddersfield and York (though probably not as breeding birds) in the 19th century. The most up-to-date information for London comes from the 1993 *London Bird Report*, published by the London Natural History Society. Observers found nearly 3,000 common gulls at Hillfield Park Reservoir, and in other places flocks of 2,000 herring gulls and up to 1,000 lesser black-backed gulls. In total in mid-winter there are thought to be about 250,000 gulls roosting on London's reservoirs. Eight pairs of herring gulls nested in London – in Camden High St, Euston Rd, Kings Cross, close to Regent's Park, St Pancras Churchyard and Whitehall. Four pairs of lesser black-backed gulls bred and six pairs nested in the same areas.

In the Midlands the *West Midlands Bird Club Report* for 1992 indicated that there have been as many as 3,000 black-headed gulls in the winter on a landfill site four miles from Birmingham City centre, some lesser black-backed gulls in the centres of Birmingham and Wolverhampton in midsummer, and at the same

Thousands of black-headed gulls may be found on landfill sites

time four pairs of this species holding rooftop territories in Worcester. Chasewater Reservoir on the outskirts of the West Midlands has for many years provided a winter roost for thousands of gulls. On any winter afternoon small groups or single birds may be seen gliding silently north-west over the city and the Black Country towns to their watery dormitory. The assembled flock taking wing like a miniature blizzard set against a winter sunset is an awesome sight.

Gulls are quite happy to live on any sort of food, and some of our city birds may never eat fish at all; the sight of gulls forming a feathery wake behind a tractor is familiar. They are behaving on a large scale just as robins do on a small scale and snapping up hapless creepy-crawlies exposed by the plough. Increasingly they are also attracted to large rubbish dumps; even some birds breeding in their traditional coastal colonies now go inland to feed rather than flying out to sea.

This scavenging habit is standing the birds in good stead. It may be that they are taking over a niche which, in an evolutionary timescale, has recently become available to them. Up to the 17th century kites were common in city streets, especially in London. In the less sanitary conditions found then they did a good job as unpaid litter and rubbish collectors. These days the rubbish does tend to be collected by the local authority, but then it is merely moved to a different place – the rubbish dump. Here the tough aggressive gulls can hold sway over lesser species and find rich pickings. Some species specialise in robbing others of their food – common gulls for instance have been seen to get almost all of their own food by robbing black-headed gulls. Sometimes the gulls' reliance on rubbish can backfire – as in South Wales when an outbreak of botulism amongst birds was thought to have originated at their feeding tip. There is something incongruous about the pure whiteness of the gulls' plumage and their presence on some of the filthiest places humans have created.

Only about a hundred years separated the disappearance of the kites from London and the appearance of gulls. Thanks to W.H. Hudson we know precisely when gulls started to colonise inner London. It was during the severe winters between 1887 and 1893 that black-headed gulls came in large numbers as far up-river as Putney. Excited people crowded the bridges and embankments to witness this unheard-of behaviour. In 1893 two things happened to help the birds. First, the magistrates stopped people from shooting them, not because the birds were protected, but rather to protect the public from the firing of guns in the street. Second, people began feeding them. It is recorded that 'hundreds of working men and boys would take advantage of the free hour at dinner time to visit the bridges and embankments, and give the scraps left from their meal to the birds.' The following winter was again marked by severely cold weather, and it is thought that the birds only survived because of the people feeding them. Hudson himself fed gulls in London parks with sprats bought for a farthing a pound. The habit of coming into the City of London persisted, so that in 1945 R.S. Fitter suggested that this change in behaviour was 'one of the most striking developments in the history of British ornithology'.

Waterfowl are often joined by gulls on inland waters

The combination of frequent feeding by people and the gulls' own habit of stealing food does lead to supposed 'attacks' on people enjoying *al fresco* refreshments. I once had a candy bar taken from my hand by a ring-billed gull in Norfolk, Virginia, and on the other side of America the same species clusters in great numbers around an open-air fish and chip restaurant on the Seattle waterfront. The owners are happy to encourage their clients to feed the gulls, but ask that the same courtesy is not extended to the local pigeons. This is a very clear indication of the muddled thinking people apply to wildlife.

It seems as if we can now look forward to increased numbers of gulls in our towns and cities. Although not really garden birds (although the Queen's gardens at Buckingham Palace entertain gulls), they are common on playing fields and around lakes and reservoirs. This may result in a whole new set of problems for people. In Glasgow gulls had to be dissuaded from roosting on drinking water reservoirs because of the health risks arising from their fouling of the water. The authorities played gull alarm calls to put them off. At Heathrow Airport more gulls are hit by aircraft than any other group of birds. Sparrows may not take too kindly to them either because they have been known to prey on them. On the other hand they are handsome birds and their calls are evocative of seaside holidays. The black-headed gull's raucous call gave it the name of 'laughing' gull (and this is what its scientific name *ridibundus* means). Perhaps we should be prepared to be amused as well as aggravated by our new neighbours.

SWALLOWS, SWIFTS AND MARTINS

The great British naturalist Max Nicholson considered that there were eight species of bird that lived in towns because of, rather than in spite of, the conditions that they found there. Swallows, swifts and martins were three of his eight species. The habits of these birds are so similar that it is best to think of them together, and ignore the fact that although swallows and martins are closely related, swifts are only distant cousins. (Swifts' close relatives are nightjars and hummingbirds.)

All of them were originally cave or cliff dwellers who now nest on and in buildings; they all need open land for foraging; they all live on insects caught on the wing and, because of this, they all spend half the year in Africa and half in Europe. A fourth species, the sand martin, shares most of these characteristics, but does not nest on buildings and has no special affinities with towns, although it may breed in old quarries or be seen feeding over open water.

It was Cervantes who said, 'One swallow does not make a summer,' but when the first swallows and martins return in March or early April, to be followed two or three weeks later by the first swifts, then you know that at least summer is on its way. Their urgent sorties to gather insect snacks, the martins flashing their white rumps, the swallows showing their velvety blue backs, seem to represent all of the unseen, but equally busy, activities of the rest of nature at this time of the year.

These birds are the living embodiment of the conservation message 'Think globally, act locally.' Their two migrations each year, one from Africa to Europe, and one the other way, link the two continents. If you help the birds swooping around your eaves, you will be conserving both British and African wildlife. The 'Dark Continent' has more than elephants, lions and gazelles. If conditions are not right in both places, the birds will decline, and in recent years this has happened. In the West Midlands, for example, total numbers of birds seen are 90% down on a few years ago. The reasons may be many, and could include bad weather on migration, air pollution in our cities, drought in Africa, and improved dairy hygiene in this country leading to a big reduction in their flying insect food. Whatever the causes, we should take note – what is bad for the birds and animals that live with us may ultimately be bad for us as well.

House martins have been living with us for so long that they have joined that small group of animals with 'house' in their name – house spider, house mouse and house fly are others. There seems little doubt that they have changed from cliff dwellers to urban lodgers, and as a result have increased their numbers and their range. They retain the colonial nesting habit typical of cliff-nesting birds, and two or three dozen pairs may nest in a line beneath your eaves. Their nests are made from mud and dried grasses, and lined with feathers and bits of plants. The stucco decorations of Belgravia attract house martins; rosettes on the French em-

Swallows, swifts and martins catch insects in flight

bassy for instance accommodate up to four nests at a time. When they were filming 'City Safari' for London Weekend Television, Gavin Weightman and Mike Birkhead attracted police attention whilst filming these 'maison martins'.

House martins are very co-operative birds. They squabble less than most other colonial nesters, and the first and second broods of the year will help their parents raise subsequent chicks. They go out to feed in loose flocks, often over water where freshly hatched aquatic insects provide lots of easy meals, and of course they gather together in late summer to discuss their travel arrangements. They hunt higher in the air than swallows, but lower than swifts, the three species spacing themselves out vertically to avoid too much competition for their aerial plankton. House martins have been described as being parasitic on man, and in turn being parasitised by house sparrows. It is a fact that they are engaged in eternal conflict with sparrows, who seem to find martins' nests irresistible. The nests are basin shaped, with a tiny entrance hole. Sparrows will take over old nests, or will peck their way into occupied nests and throw out any eggs or fledglings before converting them to their own use. When they take over old nests there is often a dispute when the martins return in the spring as to which species is going to be in residence during the summer. A more grisly spring chore for martins results from their attempts to raise as many young as possible whilst they are here. Pairs of martins frequently return to the same nest and, therefore, have to clean out the remains of any abandoned offspring before laying their new clutch of eggs.

Swallows, like martins, are almost always found around buildings. Their nests are usually (but not always) in rather than on buildings, supported by a rafter or ledge. In some places they are called 'chimney swallows' or 'barn swallows'. The nest is saucer shaped and is constructed from the same materials as those of martins. Strangely, sparrows do not bother much about these, they will take over old ones but never seem to try to drive out resident swallows. Robins and wrens will also take them over in the winter, and may have to be persuaded to leave when the swallows return. Swallows are so at home in and around our buildings that they have been known to fly through rather than over houses to get where they are going (provided that doors and windows are left open). In addition to this they rarely rest on natural perches, such as trees, but almost always choose human artefacts like telephone wires.

The third member of this group, the swift, rarely alights, let alone perches, on anything This is one of the world's most fantastic creatures, worthy of a place in any of the ancient bestiaries.

The swift is the bird of birds, the most accomplished flier the world has ever known. Its dramatic crescent-shaped body scythes the air, sometimes more than a thousand feet up, and it has an unearthly scream, guaranteed to chill the blood. Its many names include 'screamer', 'screecher', and 'screech martin'. The scientific name for the species is *Apus apus*, meaning 'without a foot'. It does of course have two feet, but uses them so rarely that the name is quite appropriate. It is sometimes said that swifts cannot take flight from the ground, but this is not true. They have some difficulty caused by the fact that their wings are long and their legs are short, but they do manage to take off eventually.

Taking off from anywhere is not something swifts have to do very often because they live their whole lives on the wing, except for laying eggs and feeding young. They can sleep and mate in flight, and they gather the plant debris with which they build their nests in the air. They stick this together with their saliva. The famous birds' nest soup is made from cave swiflets' nests constructed in this way. (These same swiftlets use echo-location in the way that bats and moths do.) The nest is saucer shaped and is often built in a hole or crevice rather than stuck onto a building like a martin's nest. Sometimes an old martin's or even a sparrow's nest will be taken over, or a nest box may be used. Unlike martins, swifts only raise one brood of two or three youngsters whilst enjoying our summer. Their relatively long life, lived in the safety of the skies, means that they do not need to raise large numbers of offspring They have few enemies away from the nest, although a small falcon called the hobby specialises in catching swifts, swallows and martins. Swifts' nests may be attacked by the usual gang of nest robbers like cats, rats, squirrels and magpies, but otherwise they are relatively safe.

A final word about swifts' remarkable flying. It is possible that each bird flies about 500 miles a day – that's over 180,000 miles a year. A bird ringed in Birmingham was recovered twelve years later in Mozambique, so it seems that many swifts will fly more than a million miles in their lifetimes.

TITS

If most people were told about a bird which is becoming more numerous in towns and cities, builds a domed nest in the branches of trees, has a long tail (and used to be known as 'long-tailed mag' or 'long-tailed pie') and spends the winter in loose flocks of a dozen or more, they would probably think that magpies were being referred to. In fact the species concerned is the long-tailed tit. Although tits are less conspicuous than magpies, the lifestyle of these tiny animated bundles of feathers mirrors that of the larger birds in all of the ways mentioned. Another thing they share is a diet of insects, although in the case of the long-tailed tits they eat virtually nothing else. This makes them perhaps the only bird relying on a constant supply of insects that manages to live here all the year round.

Strictly speaking long-tailed tits are not tits at all, as they belong to a different family, but they are so often bracketed with the more familiar blue, great, coal, marsh and willow tits that we shall treat them in the same way. This little group of birds probably brings more delight to our gardens than any other. Songsters they are not, but their comical antics, bright colours, indefatigable devotion to their young, and willingness to feed right under our noses more than make up for this.

Three of them are amongst the most common birds in gardens. Blue tits regularly appear in every garden in the British Trust for Ornithology's Garden Bird Feeding Survey and recently great tits appeared in 98% of the gardens and coal tits in 84%.

The presence of tits has little to do with buildings, or the special conditions which species like house sparrows and feral pigeons find so amenable. Tits are woodland birds, and it is the trees, shrubs, hedgerows and orchards of suburbia within which they thrive. To these acrobatic feeders areas with large gardens are like an endless woodland edge which provides them with rich pickings. Add to this the frequent provision of nest boxes, which compensate for the relative lack of old trees with nesting holes, and the large amount of food put out for them, and it is easy to see why there is often a greater density of these birds in suburbia than in the woodlands round about.

The tits do not always repay our contributions to their welfare. In 1921 in Southampton a blue tit took the first recorded peck at the silver top of a bottle of milk. Inside it found the rich cream to its liking, and somehow the news of this discovery quickly spread through the blue and great tit world. They didn't need the information superhighway, because very soon reports of this activity were widespread. In the 1940s they extended their less welcome behaviour to entering houses and ripping up papers. These included notes pinned to walls, magazines, cartons and even lampshades. This habit seems to have died out, but the two skills have combined in a new trick: the birds are now reported getting into cartons of milk where these are used instead of bottles.

In their constant search for food tits often destroy the buds of fruit and other trees. Perhaps for this reason they have not always been welcomed in the past. There is a record of a churchwarden paying for 'seventeen dozen of tomtits heads'. The churchwarden might have been better off allowing the blue tits to be his natural insecticide. The buds lost to the birds were probably harbouring caterpillars and grubs which would have destroyed them anyway, and many more insects would survive to cause more damage without the blue tits to pick them off.

That mention of tomtits is a reminder that blue tits have many names including 'tomtit', 'nun', 'blue-bonnet', 'blue mope', 'billy-biter' and 'hickmall'. Long-tailed tits (in addition to the names mentioned above) are also called 'bottle tits' (from the shape of their nests) 'long toms', 'mum ruffin', 'poke pudding', 'huck-muck' and 'mufflin'.

The driving force behind the hustle and bustle of tits is their need for food. They are all small birds (the long-tailed tit is almost the smallest species in Britain, weighing about 8 grams /0.3 oz. compared to firecrests and goldcrests at 6 grams /0.2 oz. and wrens and coal tits at 10 grams /0.35 oz.). This means that they lose heat very quickly and must keep feeding to compensate for this. Blue and great tits will take a greater variety of food than the others, including fat-rich food like coconut, peanuts, bacon rind and suet. They get direct benefits from the food we put out. As long-tailed tits only eat insects their life in the winter is much more difficult. Only about 30% of blue tits survive the winter, and it does not seem likely that long-tailed tits fare any better.

Coal tits are great hoarders of food, for instance taking seeds out of feeders and

Tits do not always repay our contributions to their welfare

storing them elsewhere. This behaviour is deeply ingrained, so much so that it is sometimes carried to what seems absurd lengths. One bird was once observed moving half a pound of nuts from a feeder to its own storage place. This amounted to about 20 times its own body weight – the human equivalent of going to the supermarket and buying more than a ton of food in one go!

Most of the tits are hole nesters, a habit which leads to some unusual sites being chosen. When hand pumps were more common they would sometimes try to build in the cavities in the handles, and blue tits have been known to use letter boxes. This willingness to use other than natural cavities is of course exploited when we put up nest boxes. Holes in buildings may be used, and great tits will even nest in holes in the ground. Nesting material is likely to include down, hair and wool, grass and moss. Long-tailed tits demonstrate the fact they are in a different family by building their nests in the branches of trees and bushes. The nest is one of the most exquisite natural objects to be found in this country, being a tiny ball of feathers, grass, moss, lichens, and gossamer from spiders' webs. One was once taken apart and over 2,300 feathers were found woven into its fabric.

Tits lay plenty of eggs, sometimes as many as a dozen, and when the young hatch the parents have a hectic time trying time keep pace with their demands for food. From first light until dusk they sally to and fro with their beaks full of caterpillars. Every day the parents have to find hundreds of caterpillars, greenfly or other insects if their brood is to survive. Many people make the mistake of putting up nest boxes and then spraying insecticide on their garden plants, thus inadvertently condemning the young tits to death by starvation. It was once thought that long-tailed tits shared their nests, as up to half a dozen adults were often seen feeding young birds. The truth is that like some other species, such as martins and moorhens, first brood birds stay around to help with the second brood.

A lot of people assume that the blue tits they see in their garden are resident there, in effect 'their' birds. Whilst this is obviously the case when nesting takes place, it is unlikely to be so in the winter. During the cold months many birds are constantly on the move, having to search widely for food and being subject to winds and storms; the birds that come to your garden will change and as many as four or five hundred different individuals may pause to refuel at your bird table during one winter.

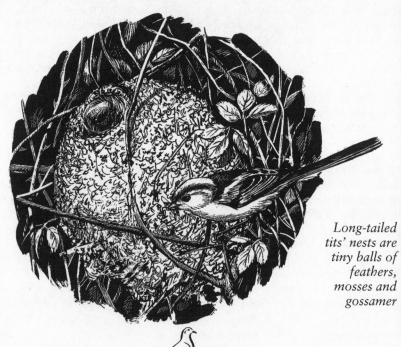

Long-tailed tits' nests are tiny balls of feathers, mosses and gossamer

BLACKBIRDS AND ROBINS

Most gardens play host to blackbirds and robins (the British Trust for Ornithology's Garden Bird Feeding Survey found them in equal second place in 99% of the gardens surveyed) and many are also visited by song thrushes, fieldfares and redwings. These birds are all members of a family which includes black redstarts, chats, nightingales and bluethroats. Some of them are amongst the sweetest songsters in the world, often imitated but never bettered by human musicians.

For two birds with such close associations with people blackbirds and robins could hardly differ more in their attitudes towards us. The ever-watchful blackbird takes alarm at the first sight or sound of human intruders into its world. As a result the blackbird's alarm call is probably the only avian warning that most of us instantly recognise. It is a sort of mellifluous chatter, given whilst winging swiftly away a metre or so off the ground. As both blackbirds and thrushes are reputed to be good to eat they may have had good reason in the past to be wary of us. Robins on the other hand positively welcome us into their domain. Every gardener has enjoyed the company of a robin, perched on some convenient point, head cocked (as if listening but in fact watching intently) and ready to descend and consume any creepy crawly unearthed by his or her labours.

As robins are the most solitary of birds, eschewing the company of not only their own kind but also other species, it seems odd that they should accompany such a different animal as us. The truth about this is not very flattering – they think we are pigs! As woodland birds preferring to eat mainly insects and worms they would be naturally attracted to disturbances of the woodland floor. In years gone by the animal most likely to be creating this disturbance would be wild boar as they rooted around for their own food. Gardening almost exactly mimics this behaviour, and as far as robins are concerned the absence of pigs is compensated for by the presence of gardeners.

The confiding nature of robins is such that once, in very severe weather, I had one perching on my hand (and hat) even though I had no food to offer it. Another robin of my acquaintance used to hop into an allotment shed to glean the crumbs left by a vixen who shared the allotment holder's lunchtime sandwiches.

The attraction of gardens for both robins and blackbirds is not only the food and water they may find but also the possibility of good nesting sites. They both nest low down, typically in a bush or hedge, or behind a creeper or honeysuckle. Robins will nest in holes, whether in old kettles or not, and blackbirds will often build their nests in outhouses and garages. I once saw one on top of an upturned broom. Another was on a pub window-sill behind a clematis. That gave the birds privacy from the outside of the building, but there was only a quarter of an inch of glass between them and the customers in the bar. Even so three young blackbirds were successfully raised.

Fledglings frequently leave or fall from the nest before they can fly. They appear helpless, and at the mercy of any passing predator such as a cat. Many people

We provide many potential nesting sites for robins

try to help these birds by taking them into care – and many of the birds die as a result! Their best chance of survival is to be left to the care of their parents, although they are not always beyond helping themselves. On two separate occasions in my garden fledgling blackbirds successfully pestered starlings for food. The starlings dutifully went around collecting worms or caterpillars and fed them to the blackbirds. Despite the comments just made about parental care, on these occasions there were adult blackbirds around who totally ignored the youngsters.

Spring is heralded in our towns and cities in various ways, some of them quite unnatural, such as the thousands of garish crocuses garnishing traffic islands. Perhaps the most beautiful signal is the singing of blackbirds. In most cities they are both the most numerous songbirds and the ones found deepest in the heart of the city. In Regents Park, for example, 18 pairs bred in 1993. From chimney pots, the tops of trees, television aerials and now in pleasing irony cell phone relay stations, their wonderful song pours out at dawn and dusk. Penetrating the roar of the traffic, it lifts the spirits of hurrying commuters. When tired of composing its own tunes the blackbird will readily mimic those of others. Its American cousins, the mocking birds, are named for this ability.

Robins cannot compete in terms of mellifluousness and so they favour us with their twisty little song all the year round. Their territorial ambitions keep them singing even outside the breeding season. They only stop when they have young in their nest, this being the one time that they do not want to advertise their presence. Street lighting can result in robins singing all through the night. In Crayford one was heard, under lights, serenading the New Year at 2.00am on January 1st, 1993.

As long as we remain a nation of gardeners, constantly disturbing the ground, planting lots of berry-bearing shrubs, growing thick climbers on walls and fences, and providing lawns which hold lots of worms, then we can expect to be repaid with the sights and sounds of blackbirds and robins. Their presence is as much a result of our labours as are the flowers and vegetables we produce.

CANADA GEESE

The Canada goose is the only species of black goose that breeds south of the Arctic Circle. The fact that some of its members choose to do so in many towns in Britain and North America should be a cause for celebration. It is not. The small wonder of birds from a remote and inhospitable part of the world adapting to urban life in the space of a dozen generations is forgotten in the welter of complaints about them.

The poor geese are unpopular because they prevent native waterfowl from breeding, foul the shores of lakes and pools, destroy waterside vegetation, steal crops of winter wheat and pollute the water with their droppings. They are shot, described as yobs, and have their eggs stolen and replaced with dummy eggs. This seems most unjust as their presence in this country is almost entirely due to human activities, and their spread in the last thirty years has been partly caused by people moving them around. They do have some virtues. In small numbers people think they are attractive (which is why they were brought here in the first place); they apparently make a 'sporting' target for hunters, and they are edible. The main one, however, may be the breath of wilderness they bring to the rush hour, as they swoop low over traffic in 'V' formation, honking just as their ancestors used to in the frozen Arctic wastes.

They are social animals, often nesting close together. Where they can they will build on islands to protect themselves from foxes and other predators. If no islands are handy they will do without. A few hundred yards from Birmingham's palatial International Convention Centre there is a stretch of canal without tow paths. In the spring Canada geese nests are built every 60 to 70 metres

along the water's edge. The nest is a paltry affair for such a large bird: a depression in the ground lined with grasses, reeds, leaves and feathers. They lay 5 or 6 off-white eggs on which the female sits for about 28 days. A goose in Birmingham once laid an egg in a swan's nest and the swans successfully raised the gosling with their own brood.

Their diet is what gets them into trouble. They only eat plants, and like nothing more than to graze on short grasses or young wheat. That is bad enough, but, being birds, they have an additional problem. Animals that eat only plants either have to eat a lot to get the nutrition they need, or they have specially adapted digestive systems. Cows sitting chewing the cud are putting the grass they eat through their complicated digestive systems. Rabbits eat their grass twice, consuming their own droppings after the grass passes through them the first time. Geese have to be able to fly, which means they must be lightweight and cannot carry either extra bits of digestive system or a load of undigested food. Therefore they need to consume a lot of food. A lot in at one end means a lot out at the other. An adult goose can produce nearly a kilogram of waste a day. A flock of 300 can produce a ton in four days. In the Arctic tundra this probably goes unnoticed, but in your local park it is very obvious.

What then caused this clash of incompatible lifestyles – those of 20th-century town dwellers and a harmless bird that lived for millions of years in harmony with its environment? In the seventeenth century early travellers to North America thought the birds attractive and brought some back to England. The first recorded Canada geese in Britain were in King Charles II's collection in St James' Park in the 1660s. Some were also taken to Louis XIV's court at Versailles. This of course made them fashionable at a time when the British landscape was about to be transformed by landscape designers such as Repton and 'Capability' Brown. Soon many ornamental lakes boasted a flock of Canada geese. By the end of the eighteenth century they were common on country estates.

The first known escapes from these flocks were in 1731. By 1845 they were described as 'free flying' in eight counties, from Yorkshire to Cornwall. In 1885 a pair nested at Edgbaston Pool, which still exists, a couple of miles from Birmingham city centre. People still thought well of the birds, and they were being introduced to new places as late as 1955. This, as well as the suitability of the English landscape, with its many lakes for breeding and fields for feeding, and the shortage of predators (only foxes pose much of a threat, and at the end of the nineteenth century they were in short supply) gave the geese a launching pad. The only question: when would they take off?

The answer – the mid 1950s. In 1953 there were estimated to be 3,000-4,000 in this country; in 1969 there were more than 10,000; in 1976 there were 19,000 and in 1990 there were 60,000. If they continue to increase at the current rate their population will double every five years. As though we had learned nothing from the past,

Canada geese can disrupt airline schedules

flocks were transported to new areas in the 1960s as an attempt to control their numbers! Just to help them a little more this was also a time when many old gravel pits were flooded, and provided the geese with yet more habitat. Canada geese are a living example of what may be called the Sorcerer's Apprentice Syndrome.

Having first of all loved them, then hated them, we are now being sentimental over them. They could be controlled relatively easily, even now, but we do not have the stomach for it. For about a month in June and July the birds are flightless because they are moulting. It would be very easy to round up large numbers and kill them. This is against our instincts as a nation of animal lovers, and is illegal unless a licence can be obtained. The law does not allow a licence to be issued to control geese damaging property or blighting amenity land. You can apply for a licence to kill geese in order to protect other species of wild birds, to preserve public health, air safety, or to prevent damage to commercial or agricultural interests. We do allow them to be shot from September to January (that's sport, so it is permissible), we addle their eggs and put them back in the nests to prevent them from breeding, we form working parties and committees to discuss the issue (there is a London Canada Goose Working Party) and string wires along the shores of ornamental pools to try and discourage them.

The current notion is to try to limit the amount of short grass beside large lakes, and instead to encourage habitats suitable for other wildlife.

It seems that whatever we do the geese are now permanently established here. They have already forced an airliner to return to Heathrow Airport and disrupted Henley Regatta – with flocks of 300 or more birds now commonplace it seems inevitable that they will continue to make their presence felt.

FERAL PIGEONS

This is yet another rock- and cliff-dwelling bird which now makes its home in the canyons of the city. In fact the feral pigeon is so well suited to city life that it is far more numerous and widespread than its wild congenitor, the rock dove. Town centres all over the world have been colonised by this much maligned, softly spoken, grey-suited citizen. Like its human companions it gathers in small groups to eat and drink and conduct the day's business. When the males want to attract the notice of the females they strut along the pavements, puffing out their neck feathers as if they are parading the latest fashion – carefully avoiding the feet of young people doing exactly the same thing.

Not many people have a good word to say for the poor old pigeon, but a species which has been exploited by humankind for thousands of years deserves better. No one is quite sure when the mutual benefits of living together became apparent, but it could all have started when we still lived in caves. Then it was the people who encroached on the pigeons' territory rather than the other way round. It is known that pigeons were domesticated 6,500 years ago in Mesopotamia. They probably came to Britain's towns (as domestic birds) with the Romans, although wild birds were probably living as they do now on the rocky north-west shores of Scotland and Ireland. The birds were so highly regarded by the Romans that slaves had to chew bread before it was given to the pigeons. Since then they have been kept for food, for entertainment (as racing birds, 'fancies' and tumblers) and for communications. In return we have fed and housed the pigeons, sometimes deliberately and sometimes, as now, unwillingly.

The ancestors of the flocks of pigeons adorning rooftops and ledges were the occupants of the dovecotes which many large houses kept until well into the 19th century. The birds provided fresh meat in the winter, and fresh eggs all the year round. In London about a hundred years ago it was noted that many birds were living in the streets and parks rather than their dovecotes, and it was thought that something ought to be done about them. So far the birds seem to be winning the war! Interestingly, even today's birds prefer Victorian buildings, with their ornamentations and embellishments, to modern glass and concrete blocks. It seems they find them easier to gain a foothold on. Even so, I once saw a Parisian pigeon perched on the 'A' in a neon sign saying CHANGE rather than on the ornate

People and pigeons strut along city streets

balcony above. On this occasion a change was good for a rest.

The next time you are side-stepping the pigeons down your local High Street you may like to consider some of their more impressive attributes. For example both males and females produce a type of milk on which they feed their young, or squabs. This milk is made in the birds' crops, and is regurgitated for the squabs to take from their parents' bills. This characteristic is almost unique – only emperor penguins and flamingos share it. Then there is their renowned ability to find their home roost from long distances away. This has been used for thousands of years – the results of races in the very first Olympic Games were carried by pigeons, and Roman emperors also used them to deliver messages. A less spectacular but very unusual attribute is pigeons' ability to drink without lifting their heads; most other birds take up a drop of water and then lift and tip their heads to swallow it.

The success of pigeons here is partly explained by another unusual feature of their biology. They do not have a breeding season, instead they are able to breed all the year round. There are about 300 species of pigeon in the world and they all lay only one or two eggs at a time, but feral pigeons can do this as many as ten times a year. There is, therefore, a continuous supply of new birds to replace those that die – naturally or otherwise.

Because of the mess they cause and the diseases they carry many birds are killed by local councils, and they must cost local taxpayers tens of thousands of pounds a year. The fact that a small number of those taxpayers like the pigeons so much that they feed them does nothing to keep the bills down. Feral pigeons seem to be able to survive on left-over bread, cakes and fast food. They scurry between the feet of shoppers gleaning what they can from pavement cracks, queue up in the park at lunchtime for sandwich box scraps, and scavenge on rubbish tips. They are probably more divorced from their natural diet than any other bird or animal, except of course for their human companions.

The use of pigeons for carrying messages, and for racing, exploits their ability to find their home roosts. It is rather curious that pigeons should have acquired such a high reputation for their homing skills: they are by no means amongst the best birds in the world at travelling. Wild rock doves do not even migrate. Racing birds and carrier pigeons operate over relatively small distances – up to about a hundred miles. Other species find their way just as accurately over much greater distances. For example Manx shearwaters which breed on the island of Skokholm spend the winter 6,000 miles away off the east coast of Brazil, and then return to their tiny island for the new breeding season. Black redstarts, which may share a rooftop perch with pigeons, travel hundreds of miles south for the winter and then return to their natal nest sites the following year. Unlike many other birds pigeons cannot find their way at night, or in the day if the sun is obscured by cloud. This is thought to be because they navigate by comparing the angle of the sun with the horizon, by means of a special part of the eye, called the pecten. This grows from the retina and may act for the bird as a sextant does for human navigators. Pigeons having more limited homing abilities than is generally realised explains why flocks of feral pigeons often include racing pigeons which never made it home. These birds can be recognised by the rings on their legs.

Their association with people may go back thousands of years, but pigeons' association with birds of prey goes back much further. They are plump birds and make good meals for peregrine chicks. Even kestrels, which are not much larger than pigeons, will take them. The instinctive fear that pigeons have of falcons has been used in control programmes as an alternative to shooting or poisoning. The managers of the Broadgate development at Liverpool Street Station, and the new stadium built for Wolverhampton Wanderers Football Club, have both enlisted the help of falconers to keep pigeons away from their shiny new buildings. The falconers fly their captive birds around the buildings and the local pigeons are motivated to go and cause a nuisance elsewhere. In Birmingham's wholesale market a sparrowhawk has been tried, but the scheme was abandoned when a member of the public was startled by a pigeon which crashed into a nearby window closely pursued by the sparrowhawk which also hit the window. In some places models of birds of prey, such as peregrine falcons, have been used to deter the pigeons.

The battle between those who welcome the presence of these remarkable birds and appreciate their virtues, and those who see no good in them and object to bird droppings on streets, statues and stately buildings, will no doubt continue. It seems unlikely that anyone will succeed in eliminating feral pigeons from the world's cities. Someone will be keeping an eye out for them, and following in the footsteps of the people in the 1950s who called the police to complain when a peregrine falcon appeared around St Paul's Cathedral and started helping itself to pigeon lunches.

KESTRELS AND PEREGRINE FALCONS

Birds of prey are wildlife stars. Other hunter-killers, whether furred or feathered, are persecuted and complained about, but – gamekeepers apart – hawks and falcons are almost universally admired. The most powerful species, such as peregrine falcons and goshawks, have traditionally been pets of the nobility.

Today the only wild bird of prey that many people see is the kestrel. In the last fifty years it has become a common sight in our towns and cities. It is unmistakeable hovering against the wind, tail fanned, wings outstretched and head held rock steady. It may also be seen swooping elegantly between tall buildings, perching on lamp-posts and towers, and strutting on the short grass of parks and golf courses. Many travellers on motorways are familiar with roadside kestrels hovering about 12 metres (40 feet) in the air over the wide verges.

Kestrels are small falcons, cousins to peregrines and sakers. Ours, sometimes called the 'Old World kestrel', is found in Europe, Asia and Africa. It is one of thirteen species of kestrels which collectively are found in many parts of the world. Like other successful town dwellers they are adaptable, especially when it comes to food and lodging. Country kestrels feed mainly on mice and voles (as probably do the motorway haunting birds) but urban kestrels feed mainly on birds, and house sparrows in particular. A study in Manchester in 1980 showed that birds formed 76% of kestrels' diet, rodents 22% and worms and insects 2%. Individual birds will tackle almost any small animal that comes their way. Their victims have included pigeons, starlings, black redstarts, rats, adders and crabs. When insects are abundant in late summer kestrel parents mimic humans by taking their offspring for picnics in the park. Families of four or five birds may be seen on the ground snapping up crane flies and other goodies.

The kestrel seen eating crabs was of course a coastal bird, and this may be a clue to the kestrel's success in towns. They are, for example, not really nest builders, preferring to find a hole or secure ledge in or on which to lay their three to six eggs. Cliffs suit them very well and so, therefore, do buildings. In London they have nested on the Houses of Parliament, Nelson's Column, and between the dragon's wings on the weathercock of Bow Church in Cheapside. Apparently the weathercock continued to turn whilst the nest was there, so for the chicks this may have been London's first revolving restaurant. The spaces behind weatherboarding on houses sometimes provide a cosy niche within which to secure a brood. Kestrels nesting in trees will usually have taken over an old nest built by another bird, typically a crow or magpie.

No one is quite sure why kestrels have returned to our cities following a decline in their numbers in the 19th century. In the early 1900s they were a rarity in towns, but returned to breed in Greenwich in 1928 and in Hammersmith in 1931. The increase since then may be linked to wartime bomb damage. The open spaces

Kestrels have nested on Nelson's Column

Town centres could have been designed to attract peregrines

created by bombs were rapidly colonised by plants such as willowherbs and daisies which produce a lot of seeds. These seeds attracted small birds such as sparrows and finches, which in turn provided easy pickings for the kestrels.

London Wildlife Trust's 'Kestrel Count' in 1988 revealed that 223 pairs were breeding in the capital, and the true number is thought to be about 400 pairs. The abundance of food and nesting sites means that there is probably a higher density of kestrels in major cities than in the surrounding countryside.

Whatever the reasons, perhaps we should just celebrate the fact that we can enjoy kestrels, or 'windhovers', as we go about our business, and reflect that if they, as animals at the top of the food chain, continue to thrive then the urban environment cannot be all bad.

Their more powerful relatives the peregrine falcons are amongst the aristocrats of the bird world. In their diving attack, or stoop, they may reach speeds of over 150 mph, making them the fastest moving creatures in the world. Like other birds of prey they suffered a major decline in the middle of this century. In the war they were killed because of the danger they presented to carrier pigeons, and immediately afterwards they were affected by the widespread use of poisons like DDT.

The population is now expanding, and as a result so is the area within which they may be found. The name 'peregrine' means wanderer, and birds do travel over many miles. This is travel rather than migration. Young birds are moving east from their strongholds in the west of Britain. In the West Midlands sightings of peregrines have risen from virtually none in 1979 to nearly 80 a year in the early 1990s. Town centres could have been designed to attract these wandering birds, and to entice them to stay. The tall buildings are just like the rocky cliffs where they like to breed, and the feral pigeons are the same species (rock dove) which they have been eating in their rocky domains for thousands of years.

In the USA captive bred peregrines have been brought into a number of cities, and have now established themselves as 'wild' birds. The first introductions were made in Washington DC in 1979. Strictly speaking they are feral falcons, just as the pigeons they eat are feral pigeons. This distinction is irrelevant to the people who enjoy their spectacular aerobatics amongst the pinnacles of human power. The waterfront development in Baltimore (the model for London's docklands) hosts a pair which nest on the top of the highest building there.

The process of establishing the falcons is called hacking. Young birds are placed on top of high buildings before they can fly, in large boxes such as tea chests. Humans act as surrogate parents, supervising and feeding the birds until they can look after themselves. About a dozen chicks need to be released over two years to ensure one breeding pair establish themselves. Although the rooftop refuges protect them from natural predators, other dangers, like plate glass windows and wires, cause the deaths of up to eight out of ten of the young birds. Hacking has become very popular. In Ohio for example a co-ordinated programme has seen birds introduced to five cities – Akron, Cincinatti, Dayton, Columbus and Cleveland. Whether or not similar programmes are tried in the United Kingdom it seems likely that peregrines will eventually start to breed in our city centres. Single birds frequently appear in and around city streets now, cause havoc amongst the pigeons and then move on.

Sparrowhawks are also taking an increasing interest in towns; they, to a lesser extent than peregrines, will also take pigeons.

HOUSE SPARROWS

A door opens, the householder comes into the backyard, there is a great whirring of wings and a dozen one-ounce bundles of feathers head for the nearest bush, from the safety of which they scold the householder, their chums and the world in general. Anyone who is host to a gang of sparrows will be familiar with this scene. If a town garden only has one species of bird in it the chances are that the species will be the house sparrow.

Thanks to urban living house sparrows are probably the world's most familiar birds. Somehow they have moved from the African savannahs of their ancestors to our houses and gardens. They may now be found anywhere in the world where there is human habitation. So closely are they associated with people that it is doubtful if any house sparrows live entirely away from humans. Their very name – 'house' sparrow – indicates how closely connected with us they are. And we like them. The first sparrows were taken to America because they reminded people of life in Europe. They were taken on wagon trains as the pioneers moved west. From the eight pairs released in Brooklyn in 1850 to the millions living from Canada to Mexico today, they have been just as much part of the wild west as cowboys, six-shooters and that other introduced – but more domesticated – animal, the horse.

The sparrows that went west did so in cages, but generally this is not the fate of this species. A rescued sparrow was taken into a house in Victorian London, however, and lived in respectable domesticity for 18 years. It was given the freedom of the house and took to attacking one of the maids whenever she appeared. The unfortunate girl was dismissed. Whether this is a comment on the strength of feeling which even sparrows can engender, or on the social conditions of the time, I am not sure.

One of the many curious things about sparrows is that despite their liking for our homes and gardens they seem never to trust us. As soon as a human intrudes into their lives they make for cover. That cover is almost always vegetation – a tree, bush, or creeper clinging to a wall. They rarely fly up to chimneys or roof tops for refuge. In fact sparrows are not inclined to fly much at all. It seems that they do so as much as necessary but as little as possible. They make short urgent little sorties between their refuges and the next meal, or from their rooftop nests to drink from a pool, but otherwise indulge less in flight than almost any other small bird.

They do prefer to nest in buildings rather than trees or bushes. This may just be laziness. If they can find a hole in brickwork, or beneath the eaves, they will make an untidy cupped nest, with wisps of straw or grass sticking out of it which never really looks finished. In trees they build an almost globular nest with an entrance hole in one side. This is presumably a lot more trouble. These nests betray their affinity with weaver birds rather than with the finches which many people think are their nearest relatives. Although individual nests are small they

will build nest upon nest. I have removed miniature haystacks from lofts with the latest nest perched on top of the previous twenty years' debris. They line their nests with feathers, but, not being too well blessed with these themselves, they will rob other birds of theirs. There are tales of sparrows taking feathers from pigeons, and I have seen them go up to sleeping mallards and help themselves to their plumage.

Having made their nests or, as often happens, taken over a martin's nest (occupied or not), the hens will lay four or five whiteish eggs, speckled with brown and grey. The hens also frequently lay in other sparrows' nests. Two or three broods a year are normal, but four or even five are not unknown. Eggs are incubated for about two weeks, and the nestlings are fledged in about another two. The main breeding season is March to August, but in this country sparrows can breed all year.

Their breeding success is partly dictated by the availability of insects or other high protein food. Although adults are almost wholly seed eaters the young do need insects or other animal matter to provide them with enough protein. (Birds that are regularly fed with kitchen scraps will be seen to eat almost anything, but bread, cake and other foods made from grain are the favoured foods.) Sparrows have been seen using car radiator grilles as mobile bird tables by gleaning the squashed insects from the bars. Some birds have discovered that sitting by garden pools in midsummer and waiting for dragonflies to emerge is an easy way to grab a takeaway. It is said that in Persia many years ago sparrows were used to hunt butterflies, and they will chase and catch these and other insects.

Life for a sparrow is not as easy as it may sometimes appear. Sparrowhawks have not been given that name for nothing and these and other birds of prey are always on the look-out for their next meal. Domestic cats are a constant hazard. Even with the extra warmth of towns, and the food put out for them, winters are

Martin's nests are desirable residences for sparrows

dangerous. A bird's weight may go down by 4% overnight – the equivalent of a twelve stone person waking up nearly half a stone lighter than when they went to sleep.

The British Trust for Ornithology's Garden Bird Feeding Survey shows that in recent years there has been a decline of one third in sparrow numbers. The RSPB's Garden Bird Survey reports that 'numbers have fallen sharply'. There are only half the numbers there were 15 years ago. In rural areas changes in farming practices may explain the drop, but there have been no obvious changes in towns and gardens which would affect the lives of sparrows. Perhaps they are telling us something we ought to take notice of.

MAGPIES

Thought of as either a burly bully-bird or a dapper delight, the 'piogen' of the Ancient Britons is a winged paradox. It is the living embodiment of our ambiguous feelings toward wildlife. One of the few birds to be the subject of hate mail in our newspapers, yet a successful and handsome suburbanite. Whilst we spend much effort in encouraging species to thrive which obviously struggle to do so, we denigrate those, like the magpie, that succeed in spite of our efforts to stop them. It is perhaps fortunate that magpies are native to Britain. If they were an introduced species who knows what venom would be directed towards them? Superstitions about magpies are summarised in the rhyme which begins

> One for sorrow, two for joy,
> Three for a girl, four for a boy.

There are a number of reasons for their low status. For a start they are a sort of crow, and all members of that family are persecuted for a variety of reasons. Secondly they do take nestlings and eggs of small birds during the nesting season. So, as it happens, do many other things, including squirrels, cats, other birds, stoats, weasels and hedgehogs. Thirdly they are very prominent. They do not skulk around at night and stealth is unknown to them. They are big, bright and brash. If they go into a blackbird's nest the whole neighbourhood knows about it. Finally they have a bad reputation – and that is a difficult thing to shake off. If Rossini had written an opera whose title mentioned their appearance – *The Handsome Magpie* – rather than one about their likeness for bright objects – *The Thieving Magpie* – they might be more popular.

Their attacks on small birds are what most concerns people. They think that magpies are responsible for wiping out local populations of birds such as blackbirds, robins and warblers. The truth of the matter is that the success, or otherwise, of birds like these depends on a huge number of factors in their environment. A pair of magpies is seen in the area, a lack of small birds is noted, the magpies are blamed. In May and June the frosts and snow of January, which may be the real reason the small birds are not there, are forgotten. A cat may well kill parent birds, leaving fledglings stranded. Magpies are more likely to kill the fledglings, leaving the parents to raise another brood. In these circumstances the cat has a greater effect on the population concerned. We should welcome the sight of magpies. As they are at the top of the food chain more magpies generally means more of everything else. And the presence of magpies does not normally depress songbird populations.

The question is often asked, 'Why the big increase in magpies in towns and cities in recent years?' The real question should be, 'Why were there not more magpies in towns and cities earlier this century?' Their history in London will illustrate the point.

In the Middle Ages magpies were well regarded, at least amongst the gentry. Tame birds were kept as amusing pets. Up to the early part of the nineteenth century they remained common in London. Writing in 1898 W.H. Hudson said that in the first part of the nineteenth century magpies were more numerous in the royal parks than they were when he wrote 'in any forest or wild place in England'. He records that they bred 'probably for the last time' in Kensington Gardens in 1856, and in central London were reduced to just four individuals which had escaped from captivity. They do not even merit a mention in Richard Fitter's *London's Natural History*, published in 1945. In 1951 Max Nicholson described them as mainly woodland birds which seemed to be becoming farm birds. During and since the Second World War magpie numbers have increased throughout the country. They are now common in London (and in many other towns and cities) having bred in central London again in 1971.

Was it persecution or some other and more subtle environmental factor that caused their decline in the metropolis? And what has brought them back? Persecution is an unlikely cause of their 115-year absence. A dedicated destroyer of magpies in Yorkshire killed 4,500 in his locality in four years, and they are as numerous as ever there. In Lund, Sweden, the police force are encouraged to shoot magpies. They have been doing this with some enthusiasm for years and there are still magpies to shoot. (In Sweden and Norway as a whole they are now more common in towns than in the countryside.) Eradicating a species from an area is a complicated business which needs more than mere murder to succeed.

Environmental factors are a more likely answer. In other parts of the world magpies are closely associated with people. For example in the last century in Drontheim, Norway, they frequented houses, feeding around them, sometimes going inside in search of morsels and nesting in the eaves, as well as on churches and warehouses. A far-sighted writer (the Reverend F.O. Morris, writing in 1857) suggested that if they were not molested they would 'naturally frequent the habitations of men'. It would seem, therefore, that modern British magpies are reclaiming habitat, familiar to their Scandinavian cousins and to their ancestors, that for some reason failed to support them for a time. Let it be hoped that the Metropolitan Police Force are not given the job of their counterparts in Lund.

Magpies build domed nests of sticks, lined with mud, about 40 feet up in shrubs or small trees. This habit means that the extensive planting that has been done in the last 25 years in most of our major towns is providing them with plenty of living space. Their main food is insects, but they will take almost anything else that presents itself. In the autumn they will be seen on golf courses and in parks snapping up crane flies as they emerge. This may be another pointer to their resurgence – amenity grasslands are now widespread, and they support big populations of crane flies. Magpies will hoard food when it is abundant, usually by burying it. (Their close relatives the jays are probably the main planters of oak trees in this country because they bury single acorns, and often do not find them again.) One magpie was once observed in Regent's Park, itself observing a squirrel that was engaged in burying a urplus of salted peanuts that had come its way. Each time the squirrel left the hoard o get more nuts the magpie hopped down from a tree and dug up the ones just leposited. A potentially useful feeding habit in rural areas is that of perching on a sheep's back to pick off the ticks and fleas in its wool.

In a country populated by any number of little brown birds magpies are a spec-acular exception. The black and white of their bodies is complemented by a long tail shot with iridescent blues, greens and purples. In the winter they gather in flocks containing anything from half a dozen to over a hundred birds, strutting round our parks looking like real city gents in their dinner jackets. Perhaps we can forgive their habit of getting egg cartons left by milkmen from beneath covers, breaking into them and eating the eggs – oh dear, it's Rossini's thieving magpie again.

STARLINGS

These smartly attired, gregarious, noisy birds are familiar denizens of our gar-dens, parks and city centres. They certainly make their presence felt, whether wheeling in flocks against a fiery sunset, chattering on ledges above busy streets, or mimicking trimphones and sending unwary gardeners indoors to answer phan-tom callers. Like black redstarts, starlings feed in open areas, in their case usually grassland of some kind, and in towns they roost high up on buildings or in trees. Given the choice they will roost in trees as long as they have their leaves on. In the autumn birds often move from trees to nearby buildings, changing back again in the spring. They nest in holes in trees or buildings.

Starling numbers fluctuate over the years. For example Birmingham's fa-mous starling roost once numbered 30,000 birds; today it is virtually non-existent. A story about this decline in the local paper in 1992 produced a number of reports of other flocks in the area, but the largest of these flocks – near to Wolverhampton town centre – contained only 2,000 birds. These changes are probably due to urban ar-eas being of secondary importance to this species; they are not town birds in the way that sparrows and pigeons are. The truth of the matter is that there are far more starlings living in the countryside than in towns and cities. I have been at Leighton Moss in Lancashire at dusk on New Year's day, when so many starlings were coming in to roost in the reedbeds that they blacked out the sky in much the same way as locusts do. There must have been scores of thousands of birds, the noise of their wingbeats filling the air as their black squadrons dipped and dived over the shallow pools. For more than ten years I also watched from an eighth-floor west-facing office as Birmingham's starlings flew into the city. Their numbers did not begin to compare with the Leighton Moss birds. Even so where they do roost in town centres they are a prominent part of the local wildlife scene.

Work done by Max Nicholson in the 1920s helps to throw some light on what goes on when the day's feeding is over. He discovered that London could be divided into three zones in relation to starlings. The outside zone was in and around the suburbs where starlings came to feed during the day and either stayed to roost or flew out to the countryside to do so. The middle zone was where birds fed in the day before flying into the centre of the city to roost. The inner zone was the roosting area itself in the middle of London.

Winter afternoons are perfect for observing the birds that are attracted by the bright lights, and the following scene is acted out in many cities throughout the cold months of the year. In the suburbs, about two hours before dusk, individual starlings begin to gather in small groups. They fly in short bursts from tree to tree, chattering as they do so and attracting more birds. They perch for a few minutes before moving to the next staging post, which is always a bit closer to the city centre. The nearer they get to the centre the bigger and noisier the flock becomes. Stragglers will be seen flying fast and direct past all the staging posts until they catch up with one of the flocks. The flocks themselves begin to merge until, as if at some secret signal, they rise high into the sky and begin to perform the aerobatics for which they are famous, before dropping down again on to the ledges and cornices of banks, building societies, hotels and shops, where they space themselves out very precisely on the ledges. It is said that if a bird fails to return to its roost the space it once occupied remains empty for some time.

A lot of things about starlings are perplexing. For example they are generally seen in flocks, either of their own kind or mixed (lapwings and rooks are frequent companions) but single birds seem well able to thrive. They have become famous as town birds but they are independent of people. This is demonstrated by the fivefold increase of the starling population on St Kilda since people left the island. After being introduced to North America starlings quickly colonised large areas, yet here they only started to breed in Devon, West Wales and parts of Ireland and Scotland in the 1800s.

Starlings are hole nesters; they will take over woodpeckers' nesting sites in trees and search out crevices in buildings. Shakespeare said: 'It is a valiant flea that lives on the lip of the lion' and Gavin Weightman and Mike Birkhead have described seeing a pair of starlings nesting in the mouth of a lion statue in the grounds of Buckingham Palace. Many birds that winter here have nested in parts of eastern Europe where they are so valued as natural insect controllers that nest

Depending on the time of the year starlings will roost either on buildings or in trees

boxes are put up for them. They are not thought of as songsters, but they sing from high perches for more months of the year than most other species. Max Nicholson has them: 'warbling, whistling, chattering, wheezing, gurgling, chuckling, clicking, bubbling and even popping'. There doesn't seem to be much else they could do!

What will happen to them in our major cities is uncertain. Their recent history shows that changes are still taking place. Up to the 1890s they were common breeding birds in London, but unlike today, all of those birds wintered in the countryside. The first recorded roost in the centre of London was on Duck Island in St James's Park, and it was the subject of a letter to *The Times* on November 3rd, 1894. The first reported roost on a building was at the British Museum in 1919. In the 1940s their presence was described as 'a noticeable change in recent years', and they were being reported from other cities, including Edinburgh, Belfast, Manchester and Liverpool. As we have seen, the relatively large roost in Birmingham has virtually disappeared recently.

No doubt wherever they occur in large numbers they will be a 'nuisance' and wherever they are declining they will be 'endangered', and whatever long-term fluctuations are happening will be totally ignored.

THE TEEMING MASSES

Millions of people live in cities, but there are many more millions of insects, spiders, worms, slugs and snails. They share our homes, offices, factories, gardens and parks. The ones we see are merely the tip of the iceberg. They are mainly adults which have survived the rigours of growth and development. Many more failed to survive between the egg and adult stages. Even a lot of adults are too small to notice, live almost entirely out of sight, or emerge only at night. These great armies of creeping, flying, lurking or burrowing animals are the invertebrates or, in popular parlance, mini-beasts or creepy-crawlies.

The numbers of species and individuals present are much larger than those of all other groups of animals and plants put together. Intensive study of a Leicester garden in the 1970s discovered hundreds of species of insects. There were 88 species of hoverfly alone. Most of these have larvae that feed on aphids, and the average garden has several species and tens of thousands of individual aphids. These two groups alone therefore account for more than a hundred species and many thousands of individual insects. In six summer days a flying insect trap in my own garden caught over 3,000 insects: 74% of these were flies, 14% were parasitic wasps and 12% were from all of the other insect orders. A study of moths and butterflies in Buckingham Palace gardens (which occupy 39 acres in

Pussmoth caterpillar in defensive posture

the heart of London) revealed 343 species, about 10% of the British total. What may be a garden to you is a universe of worlds within worlds for the tiny creatures for whom it is home.

Indoors things are only slightly different. You can get an idea of just how many types of tiny insects are sharing the house with you by taking a look in the covers of any fluorescent lights you have. Many of the apparent specks of dust, seen under a magnifying glass or low-power microscope, will be seen to be dead insects. There will be little flies, moths, maybe some beetles, and probably a lot of black or brown insects with narrow 'waists' – these are some of the 5,000 or so species of wasp found in Britain.

It is difficult to categorise our relationships with these legions of invertebrates. Some species relate to humans in different ways at different stages of their life-cycles, or at different times or in different places. There is a greenbottle for example that is found exclusively in and around houses in the north of Europe, but only rarely in houses in the south. Some species just carry on living in an area after a town has developed, others thrive in the new conditions and increase their numbers as a result. Yet others have travelled the world with us and now turn up in almost every major city. Scientists have a name for all of the species that live in close association with us – they call them 'synanthropic species'. Many people think that insects and other animals have evolved to suit the conditions we have created. This is not generally so. What happened was that certain species, already having lifestyles which fitted them in advance for urban life, have done well. They have formed entirely new communities with other species with the same attributes, so that we have seen ecological and behavioural changes rather than species evolution. Nowadays house flies, cockroaches, house spiders, bluebottles and the fleas in house martins' nests could all meet in and around your house, even though their ancestors would never have encountered each other.

For convenience, and keeping in mind that the divisions are not clear-cut, we can say that there are three sorts of creepy-crawlies sharing our urban living space: **hangers on** which have stayed around after we moved in on them, typically woodland and wetland species; **thieves in the night,** able to exploit the special conditions we have created, such as those found in gardens, food stores and places like wardrobes where large quantities of originally natural materials are kept; and **fellow travellers**, moving with us on and in our bodies, clothes, baggage, plants and food.

HANGERS ON

As woodlands were cleared and marshlands were drained to make way for our towns and cities the original inhabitants had two choices – adapt their lifestyles to the new conditions or become isolated in smaller and smaller relics of their woodland or wetland homes. Many creatures fall into the second category, and the fragments of ancient woodlands dotted throughout suburbia support a great variety of insects and other mini-beasts as a result. The wetland creatures probably suffered greater direct losses when towns first developed, but with the coming of canals, and parks and gardens with ornamental ponds, have been able to make a bit of a comeback in the last couple of hundred years. Their success in recovering depends on at least two critical factors – the presence of a breeding population close to newly created water bodies, and the ability of individuals in that population to move into the new homes.

The most successful hangers on belong to the first group, those that have adapted their lifestyles. Woodland edge creepy-crawlies have probably hardly noticed the difference between their natural haunts and the flowery glades that are domestic gardens. Butterflies such as the speckled wood and holly blue, many species of moths whose caterpillars feed on plants like hawthorn, sallow, crab apple or cherry, the gall wasps that live on oak trees and the spiders that skulk in bark crevices – these and countless others find homes in our parks and gardens.

When it comes to buildings it is probably woodland beetles that have been most successful in transferring from the natural to the artificial environment. The abundance of dead wood in our homes, offices and factories, whether as roof timbers, floorboards or furniture, provides perfect habitat for the burrowing larvae of beetles – known to us as woodworm. There is very little nutrition in dead wood and so each beetle grub spends anything from two to four years reducing the wood around it to powder. When enough larvae have done this the wood weakens sufficiently to collapse, sometimes with disastrous results. The tell-tale signs are the neat exit holes made by adult beetles getting out (not getting in as many people think) and the mysterious little piles of sawdust that appear in cupboards or beneath furniture. Unfortunately the impedimenta of modern life coupled with the efficiency of vacuum cleaners means that it is very easy to miss these signs of hidden trouble as an ancient woodland denizen munches its way through a modern semi.

Out amongst the petunias and asparagus other ex-woodland mini-beasts also find an abundance of food. Woodlice for instance. These are fairly harmless creatures who just like a damp and dark spot to do all the things that make a woodlouse's life worthwhile. Their fondness for damp places gives a clue to their origins. They are crustaceans, the group that includes crabs and lobsters and many other marine animals. In fact they are the only land-living crustaceans in Britain.

There are several species of woodlouse, including the pill-bugs, so named for their ability to roll up into a ball. Being to a certain extent armour-plated (the scientific name of one species is *Armadillidium vulgare*), this seems to be a reasonable defence. Unfortunately evolution failed, in this as in so many other cases, to allow for the stupidity of humans. Because of their resemblance to pills the poor old woodlice used to be prescribed as medicine and patients were instructed to swallow them!

There is one sort of woodlouse which can grow up to 5 centimetres (2 in. long). It is found around the coast, where it feeds on rotting wood, and has turned up in the heart of London's Docklands at Woolwich. Its food would seem to naturally limit its numbers on the coast where it is in relatively short supply, but pre-adapt it for success in coastal towns and cities where jetties, docks and waterside structures in general provide an almost unlimited amount of food.

Bees and wasps are another group of woodland edge insects which now do very well in towns. They are amongst the most active, most loved and most hated insects. They are usually only seen on the wing, bees collecting pollen and nectar, wasps not only collecting pollen and nectar but smaller creatures such as greenfly and caterpillars as well. Whilst doing so both groups pollinate many plants, making them very valuable garden workers. Even so tens of thousands of wasps' nests are destroyed each year, although bees are generally welcomed, or at least tolerated.

In spring large bumble bees are seen lumbering around, often taking meals from early flowers such as willow catkins, and searching out nesting sites in holes and cavities. These are queen bees which have emerged from hibernation. Once they have raised their first batch of workers they are not seen again as they retire to their nests to do nothing but lay eggs. The workers are the smaller bees which fill summer afternoons with their gentle humming.

Many other species of bee make a good living in urban areas, including solitary mining bees. These excavate cells in the soil, in soft mortar, wood or plant stems, or take over dead snail shells, which they provision with pollen and nectar before laying their eggs. The cells are then sealed. The larvae hatch, feed on the provisions and nearly a year later emerge to repeat the process. It is these bees that make the neat piles of soil on lawns or excavate soft mortar in old walls in the spring.

Wasps have a fearsome reputation, are blamed for all manner of 'crimes' – such as spoiling fruit – of which they are usually innocent, but are generally very beneficial insects. They do build nests in awkward places sometimes – in porches and conservatories for example. I once saw the anchor point of a wasp's nest which had been attached to the underside of a wooden bed whilst the owner was downstairs having breakfast! There are about half a dozen species of social wasp in this country, and two new species have established themselves in the last few years. Two species of common wasp (which are almost identical) cause the most concern. Their nests can be as big as pumpkins and contain thousands of workers. Lofts, garages and outhouses are favourite building sites and no doubt are modern substitutes for holes in big old trees. Wasps can get lost going to and fro

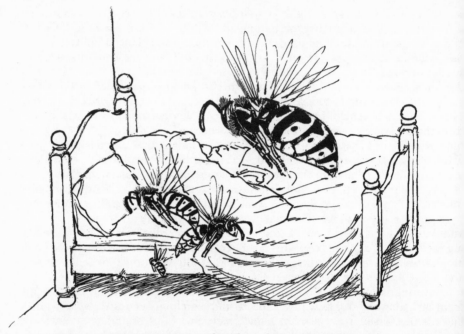

Wasps sometimes build nests in awkward places

and end up in living rooms, and sometimes the nests are too close to entrances o other heavily used places and have to be removed. They are though wonderfu structures, constructed entirely from papier-mâché made by the wasps from chewed up wood. If you can avoid disturbing the nest you will be repaid with thousand: of insect pest hunters in your garden. In the autumn both bee and wasp colonie: die out, with mostly only newly mated queens surviving the winter.

Ants are closely related to bees and wasps and are frequently found inside houses Every year sultry summer days are marked with clouds of flying ants, and jaded sub-editors run non-stories about this phenomenon, as if it had never happened before and will never happen again. Only the virgin queens and their suitors fly, and then only for as long as it takes to mate. The newly mated queens soon come down to earth (literally so) and set about forming new colonies. Paved surfaces are par ticularly good places for ants to build their nests. They make their networks o tunnels beneath the slabs where conditions are cool, dark and undisturbed, and when preparing for the nuptial flights can easily excavate exits between the slabs.

Ants are generally harmless to people, and probably do more good than harm in the house and garden. They are tireless scavengers, running, climbing, exploring and generally poking their metaphorical noses into every nook and cranny. Obvi ously unwelcome in the sugar bowl, they nevertheless tidy up many unseen corners

If they had shoulders to rub they would be doing so with the snails and slugs slithering through the strawberries. Many of these were originally woodland animals, but now one species of slug is so common around human habitation it is called the garden slug. There are nearly 90 species of land snail and just over 20 species of slug in the United Kingdom. The only major difference between them is that snails have shells and slugs do not. Most of them like fairly damp conditions and snails need calcium (a major component of limestone) to build their shells. This need for lime means that snails are often found on and around walls and from this point of view urban life suits some species very well.

Those that find themselves amongst the petunias and parsnips prefer the owner of these not to be too tidy. Neat and formal gardens provide less to eat, fewer places to hide and are often drier than more informal or untended ones. Although most snails eat unregarded left overs such as already broken off bits of plants, fungi or carrion, some species are very fond of their greens. They have a tongue that acts like a rasp on the leaves and stalks of plants, leaving them shredded and tattered. Thrushes and blackbirds may come to the gardener's aid, and large stones are often used as anvils as the birds bash open the snails' shells to get at the juicy morsel within. There are plenty of other animals on the look-out for easy meals, and hedgehogs are said to have a particular liking for slug suppers.

Slugs share with cockroaches a major public relations problem, yet most of them are relatively harmless creatures who go mainly unseen about their slug business. Unfortunately there are a few species, some of which are common in towns, that do great damage in the garden. Although slugs are mainly nocturnal, they may be seen in large numbers immediately after a shower of rain on a warm evening. Grass verges and paths quickly become dotted with slugs, especially the black ones in the genus *Arion*. Otherwise the best way to see both snails and slugs is by torchlight after dark.

Your nocturnal investigations may be rewarded with a sight of one of the most remarkable mating acts there is. The great grey slug, which can grow to 15 centimetres (6 in.), mates in mid-air. This considerable feat is accomplished when a dating pair of these slugs climb a fence, wall or tree. They find a suitable place to embrace, twine themselves around each other, and whilst so doing exude a string of sticky mucus with which they lower themselves from their perch. When suspended in mid-air they complete their mating with a mutual exchange of sperm before one of the pair climbs back up the mucus thread. The other sometimes does the same, eating the thread as it does so, or it may drop to the ground.

As well as land snails and slugs there are about 70 species of water snails in Great Britain. These do very well in towns and cities, with canals and ponds being especially good for them. Rivers and streams can also be rich in snails, but they are more likely to suffer from pollution, especially after storms, thus making them more dangerous places for snails which need clean water to thrive. The value of canals to snails is illustrated by the fact that several species from other parts of the world are now established in our canal system.

Whereas all of the land snails are single-shelled, like winkles and whelks, water snails may have one shell or two. Those with two are called bivalves, like cockles, mussels and scallops. Amongst the freshwater bivalves are the painters' mussel, so called because in times past artists used the shells for mixing their colours, and swan mussels, which can grow to 23 centimetres (9 in.) long. These may be found in the mud of ornamental ponds, boating lakes, canals and rivers. Another closely related species is the pearl mussel, a fresh water species that produces small pearls which were much valued in Roman times. At the opposite end of the size stakes are the tiny pea-shell cockles, easily taken for gravel or grit (the smallest of these is only 1.5 mm in diameter) which may be found in large numbers in ponds, rivers and canals.

Any water, even in small amounts in places like gutters, drains and water butts, provides replacement nurseries for the larvae of countless numbers of tiny flies variously called gnats, midges and mosquitoes which used to infest long since drained marshy areas, natural ponds and stream and river valleys.

Some of these flies bite us – or to be strictly accurate they suck our blood, their mouthparts acting like hypodermic needles in reverse. The females are the guilty ones, the blood providing the proteins needed for their eggs. Many species take the blood they need from birds rather than people. One of these commonly comes into houses (probably because it is attracted to dark, sheltered places where nests are more likely to be found) and keeps us awake by whining around the bedroom all night. In the winter the only sign of life in the garden apart from birds is likely to be little clouds of dancing gnats. These are males performing their aerial ballet to attract females for mating.

Another wetland fly – *Teichomya fusca* – used to be one of the most common insects in 18th century London. It had a fondness for cess-pits and carrion and was able to thrive in the unsavoury conditions of the time. Now it hardly figures in accounts of the capital's insects, although in some European cities it is said to be responsible for breeding in such vast numbers as to block sewers.

Wetland flies hanging on in suburbia are almost bound to attract the attention of their ancient enemies damselflies and dragonflies. These spectacular creatures, which breed in water, have managed to stick around even in the hearts of major cities (I have seen them in Birmingham and Milan city centres). Many of them are territorial and patrol and defend the edges of a pool or a stretch of canal. The dragonflies themselves may provide breakfasts for sparrows and other birds when they first emerge from the water. They have to crawl up a stem, clamber out of their nymphal skin and wait for their new skin and wings to harden. This turns them into fierce aerial hunter-killers, but as it is happening they are helplessly vulnerable.

While many creatures have hung on above ground, earthworms have survived under the soil surface. They may be lowly creatures, but not so lowly that they escaped the attentions of either Charles Darwin or Gilbert White, both of whom realised the importance of worms to the health of soil. Worms share with slugs the ability to digest the cellulose in plant cells, and like them get most of their nutrition from dead and decaying plant fragments.

Worms have a hard time of it in towns and cities – literally so in areas where the original soil surface is buried below successive layers of rubble from demolished buildings. They are mainly found in places that have not been built on, such as allotments, fragments of countryside, river valleys, golf courses, playing fields, parks and gardens, especially where the main vegetation is grass. They are nature's soil conditioners, acting as miniature tunnellers and excavators at, or just beneath, the surface, dragging leaves into the soil, and allowing air and water to circulate in the top few centimetres. Where conditions are right there can be tens of thousands of worms belonging to several different species. They are amongst the largest representatives of a huge army of largely unseen decomposers, organisms which take the dead and decaying remains of plants and animals and recycle them into the basic building blocks from which new plants and animals are made. Their fellow workers in this endeavour include eel-worms, tiny mites and insects, bacteria and fungi.

There is a curious link between earthworms and human settlements in the form of some little flies called cluster flies. There are about a hundred species of cluster flies in Britain, and their larvae are internal parasites of worms. They hibernate as adults, and in the autumn large numbers sometimes come into houses to pass the winter. They have a penchant for cool, quiet upper rooms or attics. What the natural habitat is that these mimic it is difficult to say, caves perhaps being the most likely.

Another familiar group of flies is that containing greenbottles and bluebottles. Greenbottles do not come into buildings very often, but they were originally woodland flies which feed on carrion. They are very common in towns and cities, and there is at least one species which is only found in association with people in the north of its range.

Bluebottles, or blowflies, on the other hand frequently enter houses, or at least the females do, in search of meat on which to lay, or 'blow' their eggs. Males are more likely to be found enjoying the delights of the flower borders, taking nectar from flowers. Again they are basically woodland species which can take advantage of a common food item, in this case meat, provided by humans. In central Europe their population density increases around forest hotels and chalets, and so they appear to be very well 'pre-adapted' for an association with us. The larvae of bluebottles are the anglers' gentles or maggots.

THIEVES IN THE NIGHT

Almost anything that started life as part of a plant or animal will be on the menu of some sort of mini-beast. We provide such food in great amounts, as with nectar and seeds in the garden, stores of grain, piles of fruit or vegetables, crops or organic wastes; or we may offer it in a greatly changed state, as with paper, glue, wool and cotton clothing, cooked meats or processed foods like cheeses. With great concentrations of these organic materials in and around our buildings it should be no surprise that hungry hordes of insects and similar creatures should be stealing the bounty.

We must expect, for instance, our flower beds to be alive with all manner of colourful creatures, zooming or fluttering from flower to flower. After all, flowers evolved in the first place to attract insects not people. We provide huge floral banquets and bees, flies, beetles, butterflies, moths and sawflies gorge themselves at the feast. In the vegetable patch white butterflies, which would not occur in especially large numbers in natural environments, home in on cabbages, and the tiny parasitic wasps which live in their caterpillars are probably more numerous now in towns than they are in remote and rural areas.

Aphids do not go for the nectar in flowers, but plug themselves into the stems of plants and steal the plant's own food as it moves through the tissues. Concentrations of different species of plants in gardens, streets and parks results in vast numbers of these tiny bugs enjoying the free feast. They imbibe more sugars than their bodies can deal with, and the excess is exuded as honeydew. Anyone who regularly parks a car beneath either sycamore or lime trees in midsummer will be familiar with the resultant sticky rain.

Taking advantage of the aphids, which are themselves taking advantage of all the plants we put in, are a number of predatory insects, especially ladybirds and hoverflies. Ladybirds also like our houses to hibernate in. They find the spaces between window frames, for instance, as comfortable as the space beneath the bark of fallen trees, and scores of ladybirds may be encountered in the winter months in suitable spots. We may have cut the trees down but in this case we have provided alternative winter quarters. Hoverflies do well in gardens because the adults visit flowers and a lot of their larvae feed on aphids.

Fruit flies, as their name suggests, occur in large numbers wherever fruit stored or processed. In warm climates they are frequent visitors to domestic fruit bowls. In this country the adults are likely to be found close to pickle factories (their other name is vinegar flies), breweries and fruit-processing plants. They may also visit your beer or wine glass in pubs and restaurants. They are small yellow/brown flies with red eyes.

There are members of two major groups of insects – moths and beetles – feasting themselves in our houses, warehouses, food factories and homes whose lifestyles are so similar that it is convenient to look at them together. About a hundred species are recognised as major pests of food factories and many of them are now

Elephant hawk moth

found all over the world, thanks to the concentrations of cereals, flour, cocoa, chocolate, nuts, fruit and textiles in our towns and cities. They share common names like clothes moths, tapestry moths, meal moths, mill moths, cheese skippers, flour beetles, bacon beetles, mealworms, leather beetles, grain weevils and carpet beetles. In most cases it is their larvae that chomp through our food, clothes, curtains and carpets. Many of the adult moths do not feed at all, so the expression 'moth-eaten' is somewhat inappropriate.

The adults lay their eggs in the foodstuffs they favour and the resulting caterpillars or grubs hatch out into an endless food supply – for them the pest things in life are free. A lot of them are able to digest the keratin in feathers and hair, and therefore things like wigs made from natural hair, feather boas and furs are all at risk. Anything else made from animal or plant fibres, such as woollens, silks and cottons may also be attacked. Modern buildings favour species liking warm, dry conditions, such as the 'woolly bear' larva of the carpet beetle, and the common clothes moth, but species liking damper conditions, such as the case-bearing clothes moth have declined. The carpet beetle is now the major household textiles pest, having wrested the number one position from the common clothes moth.

Another characteristic of these moths and beetles is that for many of them their natural habitat is bird, rodent or wasp nests. As houses are in effect big nests, and as many other creatures build their nests in and around them, it is easy to see how these insects have prospered with urban life. Sparrow, pigeon and house-martin nests may shelter hundreds of larvae, which as adults find their way from the loft to the wardrobe. Many of the moths have a metallic sheen, and when disturbed are more likely to scuttle for cover than to fly away. They prefer darkness to light, and will always move to the back of a drawer or wardrobe rather than out into the room.

With all of these mini-beasts enjoying free lunches it is a good job that another unseen army is helping to control them – the spiders. These have eight legs, separating them from insects, all of which have six legs, and they are the most well known members of a large group which includes mites, ticks and scorpions. Spiders all consist of a big body containing silk glands, attached to which are lots of legs, lots of eyes and poison fangs. They are predators who stalk, snare, entangle or ambush their victims. While you watch the latest 'superhero cleans up the city' video the spiders in your lounge go about the same business, albeit somewhat more quietly. But to some the spider superhero is a terrifying baddie.

The spiders are indifferent to our attitudes towards them. They will clean up the insect pests just the same, so people in Florida may have help with cockroaches from giant crab spiders which come into their houses, and in other parts of the world spiders may clear bedrooms of bedbugs, mezzanines of mosquitoes and lounges of lice. In Mexico there is a spider that lives in large colonies called 'living fly traps'. Their virtues are recognised and the colonies are collected and brought into houses to control flies. That spiders eat cockroaches is apt, because the first cockroaches recorded in London's cellars were seen by a Dr Muffet in 1634. Little Miss Muffet, famous for being frightened by a spider, was his daughter.

A number of species have spread themselves around the world with humans and specialise in living in buildings. No doubt some of these would once have lived in caves or big holes in trees. In Britain one of our largest spiders is found almost exclusively in buildings – so much so that it is called the house spider. To be strictly accurate two of our largest spiders enjoy this common name, as a few years ago it was discovered that this one species was actually two. It (or they) are likely to scuttle across the lounge carpet, or appear in the bath, at almost any time. There are a number of other spiders in the same genus (*Tegenaria*) which are frequently found in buildings.

Spiders attract far more fear than they merit. Many more people die from bee and wasp stings (and this is rare) than die from spiders' bites. Even so the poisons in some species (though not in the UK) can cause severe illness and even death. This is reflected in some of the names they have – such as the black widow spider. Large numbers of this species occupy a big garbage dump near New York. Most spiders do not have common names, but one of the most dangerous does have the innocuous name of the 'brown recluse' spider. One of these, practising being a recluse in a pair of slacks in a ladies' clothes shop in America, was disturbed by a customer trying on the slacks in question. It bit the unfortunate lady, a Gladys Flippo, and as a result she was in hospital for a month. The brown recluse commonly lives in buildings, and generally will not bite people. When it gets tangled in clothes or towels it is most likely to do so, and one is suspected to have been responsible for appearing from a fruit bowl at a dinner in Cambridge and making a dinner guest very ill after biting him on the leg.

Fruit bowls should perhaps carry hazard warning notices, because the speed of modern picking, packing and transport means that lots of spiders, scorpions and goodness knows what else are being jetted in a matter of hours from tropical plantation to temperate plate.

At least a South American huntsman spider, or a big Costa Rican cockroach, is easily seen. The millions of mites (first cousins to spiders) living with us are generally so small that they are overlooked, although the bright red ones which can be a pest in greenhouses are well known. Mites live in and on us and our pets, and in and around our larders, homes and gardens. More than twenty species are known from sparrow, martin, jackdaw and pigeon nests, and some live in bee and wasp nests. So far only one species has been discovered which seems to rely entirely on human activities for its own success. The species – *Gohleria fusca* – has never been found in natural habitats, but only in association with people. As if the number of real mites was not enough (I have found them for instance living inside a camera) people have even invented imaginary species, such as 'cable mites'.

One group of mites should be considered as the most dangerous wild animals in Britain. These are the house dust mites which are responsible for producing the allergens which lead to people suffering from asthma. Extracts of the allergens from mites have been found to be a hundred times more potent than in the dust itself. About two thousand people die from asthma every year, the direct cost to the National Health Service is £450 million, and the indirect cost is many times more. Despite this most people are unaware of these tiny creatures which share our houses, and worry more about being stung or bitten by bees and wasps – an often painful but rarely serious occurrence.

Back in the garden another lot of mites chomp away at our beloved flowers and vegetables. Any garden with sycamore and mountain ash trees is almost certain to have them on the leaves. On sycamore their presence is betrayed by scores of tiny red pustules on the leaves, and on the rowan by patches of what looks like pale felt. The mites' feeding causes the plants to react by producing these structures which are called galls. Big-bud disease of fruit bushes is just one of many other galls caused by mites on a wide variety of plants.

FELLOW TRAVELLERS

With this group we come to the real specialists at living with humans. Some of them turn up in almost every city in the world, most of them are thought of as pests and all of them are exploiting our lifestyles. Many carry dangerous diseases, but at the same time do us some sort of service by helping to clear up the enormous mess we make. The most familiar fellow travellers are flies, so we will start with them.

Just as there are a lot of little brown birds which are difficult to tell apart, so there are lots of little dull coloured flies. There is a species properly called the 'house fly' (although 'manure fly' would better reflect its habits) but most houses will shelter several others which may well be labelled as such. They include the lesser house fly, and the fruit flies and cluster flies mentioned earlier.

The house fly proper (*Musca domestica*) is thought to have originated in Africa and may have been one of the first species to attach itself to people. There is a theory that it arrived on these shores with the Romans, but as they were by no means the first people from mainland Europe to arrive here perhaps we should not blame them for this particular irritant. The house fly has had a rough ride this century. The invention of the horseless carriage greatly reduced its manure heap nurseries, and there are probably far fewer around now than a hundred years ago. Despised and derided it may be, but it remains one of the world's great fliers. With all of our technology we still cannot build a machine that can do what every house fly does hundreds of times every day – land and take off upside down! It flies so well because, like all flies, it is equipped with one pair of very efficient wings and one pair of little gyroscopes, or balancers, called halteres. In some species these beat 20,000 times a minute – about six times faster than engines in the average family car.

Such considerations did not stop the residents of Tokyo from swatting an estimated 117 million of them on National Fly Day in 1933! This probably caused no more than a blip in its population numbers. House flies do so well in towns because they breed in all sorts of waste, whereas their country cousins are more fussy. In the wild in the tropics and sub-tropics house flies are associated with the droppings of large grazing animals, in farmed areas they are associated with the droppings of farm animals, but in towns they are associated with organic waste in general. Add to this the warmth and shelter of buildings, compost heaps and other places which help the flies to survive the winter in their immature stages, and we have no chance of ridding ourselves of them. We can it seems add a third certainty to life – in addition to death and taxes there will always be house flies.

There will probably always be lesser house flies as well. Slightly smaller than its cousin (despite what people think little flies do not grow up to be big flies – they are fully grown when they emerge from the pupa), this is one of the most abundant flies in buildings, reaching peak numbers in Britain in July. Males of the species are the flies that zoom from corner to corner of triangular or quadrilateral beats beneath light fittings, hovering briefly before each change of direction. The females sit on the walls, presumably giving marks for artistic impression and technical merit before picking a mate.

This is one of the species that becomes more closely associated with people the further north it is found. In some places there are two apparently separate populations, one living in houses and other buildings and the other not. It may have latched on to easy urban living through its frequent occupancy of birds' nests. Its larvae are often found in sparrows' nests, and so it, the sparrows and us have probably been together for a very long time.

Just like the house fly, the lesser house fly has the unfortunate habit of moving from food to filth and back again, and therefore can transmit diseases to its human landlords. It is quick enough on its wings to have laid eggs in soiled nappies whose transfer from baby to washing machine had been delayed.

Although it does not come into buildings very much, one of the world's most widespread hoverflies is very common around human settlements. This one looks so much like a bee that it is called the drone fly. Its larvae live in water, and everywhere that people have dug drainage and irrigation ditches the drone fly has prospered. The secret of its success is that the larvae have long breathing tubes, which reach to the surface of the water and allow them to breathe atmospheric oxygen. Because of this they can live in heavily polluted water, such as the open sewers which used to characterise towns and cities. This fits them very well for life in modern towns where there is all manner of polluted water. They can breed, for instance, in water butts half full of decaying leaves. Drone flies are now found throughout America, Asia and Europe.

A largely unseen and, therefore, unknown group of flies are happily living out their lives in our living rooms, conservatories and greenhouses. These are members of the family Sciaridae, and are sometimes called root gnats. They live and breed amongst the roots, moss, and general detritus in plant pots. You probably get some free with every potted plant you buy – along with a sprinkling of springtails, a modicum of mites and a general assortment of other soil dwelling mini beasts, such as the New Zealand flatworm.

Springtails are primitive wingless insects, so named because they can propel themselves in short leaps, rather in the way of fleas. Someone has calculated that a nine inch layer of soil an acre in extent contains 230,000,000 springtails.

A near relative of the springtail is the familiar silverfish. This also lacks wings. It has three long 'tails' and because of these is in a group of insects called bristletails. One species of silverfish is invariably found indoors, especially in kitchens and bakeries. They feed on flour, sugar and even the glue of cartons, and are usually seen scuttling for cover with their silvery scales glinting. Firebrats are very similar, but seek out warmer places around hearths and ovens.

The New Zealand flatworm is a relatively new fellow traveller which is taking advantage of the homes-and-gardens culture of our suburbs. Many garden plants are now grown and distributed in pots or containers, and at some point soil has been imported containing the flatworm. It has bred and been given thousands of free lifts to suburban gardens. Unfortunately it is a parasite of earthworms, which are killed as the flatworm develops. More and more records of the flatworms' presence are coming in from around the United Kingdom and there is much anxiety for the future of the earthworm population.

Another exotic exploiter of city life, but cosy buildings rather than flower beds, is the Pharaoh's ant. This tiny species, which comes from much warmer climes, can only survive in Britain in hospitals and other large heated buildings, where the hot dry atmosphere suits it well and there are plenty of places to conceal its nests. The artificial warmth means that the ants can ignore the seasons and keep breeding all the year round. Also in their favour is the fact that each nest contains several queens. These provide a constant supply of new colonies. Controlling them is very difficult because the yellow workers are only 2 mm long, and the queens are only 5 mm long. This means that the workers can get almost anywhere, and do get everywhere – like inside hypodermic needles. It has been estimated that 20% of London's hospitals are home to these tiny insects. They apparently carry the *Salmonella* organism and have caused operating theatres and wards to be closed for disinfestation. They hitch lifts on hospital trolleys and in handbags, and have even been found in bed with patients.

The fellow travellers *par excellence* are the cockroaches. Looking something like beetles, but grouped with praying mantises in an entirely different order (and they are cousins to another domestic insect, the house cricket) they are a mainly tropical group. The cockroaches that inhabit our buildings probably originated in Africa. When they are found out of doors in this country they tend to favour artificially warm places such as rubbish and compost heaps. Like house sparrows and house mice, they have travelled all over the world with people, and could probably not survive in the cooler countries outside towns and cities.

It must be said that cockroaches have a public relations problem. This results from their willingness to eat almost anything (which is another secret of their success); this means that many things are contaminated by them, and the characteristic and unpleasant smell they leave behind. They do have their preferences of course. A school in the Midlands used to find drowned cockroaches in their blue paint pots but not in the red, green or yellow ones. It is an interesting feature of human nature that cockroaches are often named after a country's neighbours or old enemies. In Britain we have German cockroaches, in Germany this species is the Russian cockroach and in Russia it's the Prussian cockroach.

In other contexts cockroaches would be honoured and lauded. They have a claim to the oldest lineage of all living things. They are living fossils, not having changed much for 300 million years. It is another comment on human nature that the so-called fossil-fish, the *Coelacanth,* is hailed as a scientific wonder having been thought extinct for a mere 70 million years, whilst something that goes back to a time before the dinosaurs is persecuted unmercifully.

As those who do the persecuting know, cockroaches have not survived for so long without good reason. They are very tough. Their eggs can survive pickling in alcohol, the adults can withstand radiation better than we can, survive double the normal doses of sterilising chemicals, go weeks without water, eat almost anything and live almost anywhere – as long as it is not too cold. They have been flushed from televisions, clocks, the backs of fridges and telephones. A headless cockroach was once seen to revive and search out a suitable place to lay its eggs.

Two more sorts of creepy-crawlies attached (literally so) to humans are the blood sucking parasites fleas and lice. They have accompanied us on our travels more intimately than any of the other passengers. It is thought that modern sanitation and improved personal hygiene have removed these unwelcome insects from our lives. This is not so. For a start there are many species of each which do not occur on humans at all, but which cuddle up to our pets and to wild animals and birds. Strangely horses are never hosts to fleas (nor, it is said, are people who work with horses) and bats carry no lice.

You may suffer from several species of flea which will make you itch while they hitch a lift. We are true hosts to only one of these (a species which also naturally lives on pigs and badgers); the others mainly occur on other mammals, including rats and mice, and our dogs and cats, but two occur principally on birds, one of which is almost always found on starlings and house sparrows. Another species has arrived on our bodies after first transferring from the tit family to domestic fowl.

Probably we have birds to thank for introducing us to both lice and fleas. Millions of years ago when our ancestors were few in number, living in trees and constantly moving about, they suffered less from the attentions of parasites. When we set up permanent homes in caves many of these were probably shared with birds, and the chance was there for their lice and fleas to transfer their attentions to us. Even now, in return for all the provision we make for them, with nest boxes and feeding tables, they still bring us nests full of lice and fleas, as well as the moth and beetle larvae mentioned earlier.

Five different species of flea were found in house martin nests under the eaves of houses in Leicestershire. Curiously their presence was related to the surface of the walls the nests were attached to. The combination of species found in individual nests depended on whether the wall was brick, pebble-dash or stone! Other studies have revealed that some fleas prefer ground nests, some nests in bushes and some higher nests in holes in trees or walls. With such obscure factors affecting the presence and distribution of insects is it any wonder that we do not fully understand the whys and wherefores of urban wildlife?

Fleas are lively creatures, well suited to taking their chances in the city. They are amongst the half of the insect world which develops through larvae (which do nothing but feed) and pupae (a resting stage during which the larva turns into an adult which bears no resemblance to the larva). The larvae feed on detritus in nests, or in the case of the human flea the dust under our carpets. When adult fleas emerge from their pupal stage they wait for a passing potential host and leap towards it (they are stimulated to do this by the shadow of whatever is passing). Tiny as they are, fleas can jump more than 30 centimetres (12 in.). As they do so they cartwheel in the air, pushing one pair of legs out over their backs. This ensures that at whatever angle they hit the host they will stick to it.

Modern life is bad news for human fleas. The adults probably have a hard time of things in showers, baths and saunas, and do not take too well to being drenched in deodorant, perfume or sun tan oil. In addition we tend to wear thinner and fewer clothes than in times past. The latter factor is related to improved buildings and heating systems. The warm and dry conditions suit the larvae of fleas very well, as does the fitted carpet which leaves many undisturbed cosy corners for them to develop. One of the rat fleas which is able to transmit Bubonic Plague can only survive in Britain in heated buildings. Presumably the decline in the horse population in towns has also helped fleas as far fewer people are now in daily contact with them.

Fleas have much to answer for, but have at least provided us with some amusement and entertainment; lice on the other hand have no saving graces at all. They too are everywhere in the urban scene, attached to wild and domestic animals and birds as well as to people. They belong to the other half of the insect world: they develop through a series of nymphs which gradually acquire adult characteristics. This allows them to complete the whole of their life-cycle without leaving their host. Unlike fleas, therefore, they are not very mobile creatures at all, and soon die if separated from their host. What they do have in common with fleas is a thick skin, legs adapted for clinging, small or reduced eyes, no wings and small size. The eggs of lice are the 'nits' which often betray their presence.

Some lice, including the three found on humans, show a preference for certain parts of the body. We suffer from the crab louse which favours the pubic area, and the head louse, one sub-species of which lives on the head, while the other lives on covered parts of the body. Someone, blessed with enormous patience, and no doubt starting from scratch, once counted 10,248 body lice on one shirt! As with fleas, some people are never attacked by lice, and resistance to head lice increases with age. The only other animal human lice are found on is the pig.

Lice are not favoured by life in modern cities, but they do survive, and are frequently found by nurses and teachers, although the infamous 'nit-nurse' visits to schools no longer take place. This probably has more to do with budgets than any evidence that lice are disappearing.

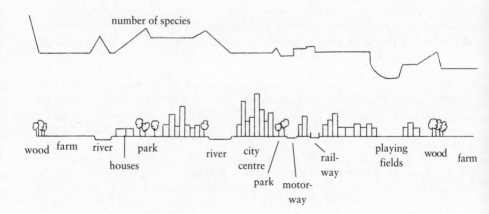

A transect from the heart of the countryside (see opposite) to the heart of a city would probably show that the numbers and sorts of invertebrates would be low in intensively farmed land, would increase where the line passed through rich habitats such as woodland or river valleys, decrease through more farmland, would increase again through the city's suburbs and then decrease as it reached the inner city and city centre. Even so I have seen dragonflies in the centre of Milan and speckled wood butterflies in the middle of Birmingham.

Honey bees

Honey bees are the only 'domesticated' insects we have in Britain. Their colonies can number thousands, and in the late spring and summer swarms of bees leave their hives to find new accommodation. These should be treated with respect and caution, but they rarely attack people. The swarm will typically be seen on a wall, or hanging from a bush or tree. It is 'parked' there while scout bees search out a suitable new home. Often the swarm will decide on a loft or chimney, or a hole in a tree. Some of them sustain themselves for years, becoming in effect feral bees.

Most districts will have a few bee keepers and they are usually willing to collect swarms and return them to their hives. The abundance of flowering trees and plants in town gardens means that urban bee keepers can get better yields of honey than their rural counterparts. For example nectar is only available for a couple of days in fields of linseed, a crop becoming more popular with farmers. Other crops like oilseed rape give a longer foraging season for the bees, but nothing compares to a garden with flowers in bloom from March to November. The abundance of lime and other trees in city streets and parks also provides a good flow of nectar.

Living together

We have seen that our towns and cities are homes not just for us but for many other animals, birds and insects. Some of these we try to wipe out (usually without success), some we tolerate (neither encouraging or discouraging them) and some we like so much that we try to attract them. In the main it is small birds and colourful insects we like to have about, but foxes, badgers, hedgehogs, squirrels, frogs and toads and bats are increasingly likely to be welcomed.

The easiest way of attracting wildlife is by feeding it. There is generally nothing wrong with doing this, but it only addresses one aspect of an animal's needs, and it is the one they probably require the least help with. The number of animals and birds in urban areas is often higher than it would naturally be as a result of the increased flows of energy. Much of this is in the form of food, whether it be discarded take-aways, the nectar in our flower beds or allotment compost heaps. Many species, such as blue tits, newts and bats, are more likely to be short of places to shelter and breed. Helping wildlife, therefore, means more than providing meals – it means trying to cater for all needs. Think what life would be like for us if we only had restaurants but no hotels – we could eat but could not rest in comfort on long journeys. And if we had nowhere to live we could not so easily raise our families.

We also have an 'attitude problem' which gets in the way when we try to cater for wildlife – we do not like the fact that half of it spends most of its time trying to eat the other half. We may like blue tits and butterflies and try to provide for both, but find it hard to accept that the young blue tits will probably be fed on the caterpillars which are the young butterflies.

There are two main reasons for our problem. The first is that we tend to see animals as if they were people, and attach human motivations and values to their behaviour. Thus magpies are accused of 'thieving' when they eat eggs, or 'murdering' when they eat young birds, but they are of course just behaving naturally. We can always find excuses for those species we particularly like, so sparrowhawks 'take' other birds, frogs 'catch' flies and kestrels 'hunt' mice and voles.

The second reason is that the welfare of individual creatures is important to us. We feel, for instance, for the young bird eaten by a squirrel, or the froglet snapped up by a blackbird. Nature on the other hand does not, it operates at the levels of populations and systems. Populations and communities of plants, animals and mini-beasts, interact with each other, and with the environment, in ecosystems. Ultimately it is the health of the ecosystems that dictates the success or failure of populations and in turn of species. To nature the fate of individuals within a population is irrelevant.

The keys to helping and enjoying wildlife, therefore, are: to create conditions which help the greatest number of species possible to complete their life-cycles; to

Animals need shelter as well as food and water

remember that in doing this they will behave naturally. Helping many species to thrive will help to ensure the success of the ones we like, even if some individuals fall prey to the ones we don't. Rather than worry about the magpies taking the first brood of the blackbirds, manage your garden so that the blackbirds can try again, and feel pleased that you are providing a place where both species can succeed.

There are four elements to this provision: shelter, homes, food and water. In many parts of the USA people who provide all of these are awarded 'Backyard Wildlife Sanctuary' or 'Wild Acres' certificates by wildlife agencies.

1. Shelter
Make sure that there are plenty of places for wildlife to rest and hide. Grow climbing plants on old tree trunks, buildings, fences and walls. Always have some long grass and slightly overgrown borders or shrubberies somewhere in the garden. The frogs, toads and newts leaving your pond need the cover provided by long grass if they are to get more than ten metres. Nocturnal creatures like hedgehogs and bats need quiet undisturbed corners to curl up in. A few piles of brushwood or old boarding are ideal refuges for the hedgehogs, and for birds like wrens. Put up bat boxes so that your local bats have somewhere to spend the day while they recover from their nocturnal exertions. Do major jobs when they will cause the least inconvenience to wildlife – clean your pond out in late summer

when the year's tadpoles have left and their parents have not yet settled down to hibernate in the mud at the bottom, avoid trimming hedges while birds are feeding young. Try to vary the height of your trees, shrubs and flowers. Different birds favour low, medium and tall vegetation. Plant conifers as well as deciduous trees, have hedges rather than fences. Let a few piles of leaves build up in unseen corners and let some plants, especially those with hollow stems, stand over the winter. Have both dark and light corners, and do not be too houseproud in the garden shed or garage. Clean them up too often and you destroy ideal spider territory.

2. Homes

Leave a few cracks and holes in walls, so that the bumble bees returning in the spring can build their nests and stick around to pollinate your fruit. Better still build a bee wall with those house bricks having lots of holes. Those same holes may also provide lodging for spiders, especially the *Amaurobius* spiders which surround the entrances to their retreats with long strands of sticky silk webs. Let some of your tall herbaceous plants stand through the winter, their hollow stems will be home to moth, beetle, fly and other insect larvae.

You can help to make up for the shortage of big old trees full of nesting holes by putting up bird boxes. Make sure they are not in the full glare of the sun, or within reach of the local cats (which, incidentally, account for far more wild birds than do magpies) and have open-fronted boxes as well as ones with holes. It will not only be nesting birds that use these – bees and wasps may build their nests in them, and small birds like wrens may roost in them in the winter. No matter what provision you make birds are likely to pick unexpected places to build their nests. I know of a nest box which regularly has a spotted flycatcher's nest on the lid, and upturned brooms in sheds or quiet corners often support blackbirds' nests. Larger animals such as hedgehogs can be provided with hibernation hotels, and foxes will be happy if there is a space for them beneath a shed.

Swallows, martins and swifts can all be encouraged to nest by giving them a helping hand. Swallows like cool, dark places inside garages or outbuildings. They can get in and out through openings as small as 5 x 7 centimetres, so a partly open door or window, or a hole under the eaves, is ideal. The birds need some sort of platform: a high shelf, or a specially made ledge will do nicely. Swifts nest just inside the roof spaces of houses and other buildings, but single storey buildings are too low for them to take flight. You can make or buy swift nest boxes designed by the British Trust for Ornithology, and special tiles are currently being developed. Martins also nest on buildings and again special nest boxes can be bought. They need mud for nesting material so to attract martins there must be a pool or stream nearby which provides this. That pool may in turn be home to innumerable insects and other mini-beasts, as well as frogs, toads, newts and snails.

A bird's-eye view of a wildlife garden

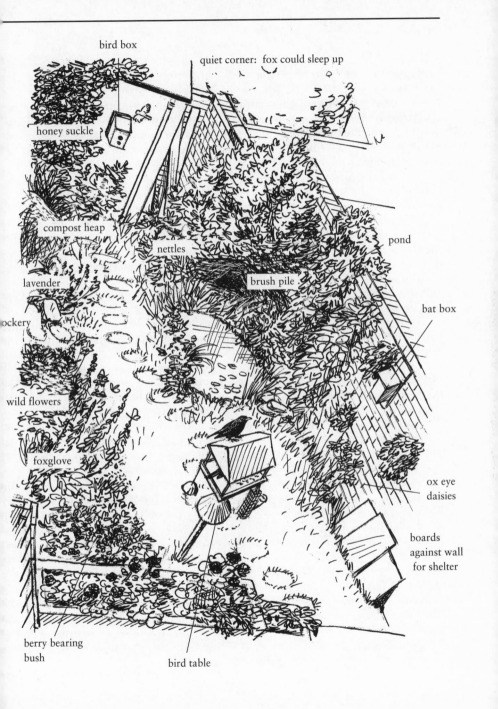

bird box

quiet corner: fox could sleep up

honey suckle

compost heap

nettles

pond

lavender

brush pile

rockery

bat box

wild flowers

foxglove

ox eye
daisies

boards
against wall
for shelter

berry bearing
bush

bird table

3. Food

There can be a lot more to feeding wildlife than putting out nuts, seeds and scrap for birds, squirrels or foxes. You can do much better than this just by managing your garden in a wildlife-friendly way. For example the more native flowers, shrub and trees you grow the more insects and other creepy-crawlies you will feed, and in turn they will attract predatory insects, birds and small mammals. Avoid growing sterile varieties of flowers without nectaries and which do not set seed. F1 hybrids are often like this.

To keep the menu tasty try to avoid using pesticides. They may help in some situations in the short term, but they break into and distort natural cycles and systems in ways which will diminish the wildlife value of the places they are used If you have problems look for more friendly alternatives. For example try companion planting of aromatic plants like marigolds alongside vulnerable vegetables such as carrots to fool the carrot fly, or put out beer-filled pitfall traps for slugs – this has the added benefit of giving your hedgehogs a tasty supper, rather than poisoning your blackbirds and thrushes with slug pellets.

Grow plenty of fruit- and berry-bearing trees and shrubs. Leave some of the fruit and berries on the branches, and leave a few windfalls where they lie. Many winter visitors like brambling, fieldfare and redwings rely on being able to find berries and fruit all through the winter. If you have spoiled or bruised fruit in the house throw it into the garden rather than the bin.

If you do feed the birds use a number of different places rather than just one bird table or feeder. This spreads the birds out, making it more difficult for the local cats to home in on them, gives the less aggressive birds a chance to get their share of the goodies, and prevents a build-up of stale food that might attract less welcome wildlife like rats. Offer food in a variety of ways – on a table for starlings, sparrows, robins and blackcaps, hanging in containers for tits, woodpeckers, siskin and nuthatches, on the ground for thrushes, dunnock and blackbirds, in seed trays attached to window sills for sparrows, tits and even wood pigeons. You can push nuts or peanut butter into bark crevices for nuthatches. Some people recommend grinding and chopping hazel nuts, chestnuts, acorns and beech mast, but this seems to be an unnecessary exercise – why not leave these where they are and let birds like jays, or squirrels, find them for themselves. Similarly it is sometimes advised to collect berries and fruit from your garden or local hedgerows, and transfer this to your bird table – again this seems pointless, you will merely be moving food from one place to another, not providing anything new. You can indulge in *haute cuisine* for birds with suet puddings and seed cakes, or provide insect food like mealworms and ants' eggs. The favourite, at least amongst the human providers, is peanuts, either in their shells or loose. If you buy peanuts for the birds (and squirrels) make sure that they are from a supplier displaying the Birdfood Standard motif. Without this there is a risk that the nuts will contain poisons which will harm the birds and mammals.

Water

If you can only do one thing for wildlife that one thing should be to supply water. A garden pond is good, but, as with food, variety of provision is ideal. Many things live in water of course, so perhaps we should have included it in 'food' above, because of the thousands of snacks provided by gnats, tadpoles, water fleas and froglets. If possible have deep and shallow, running and still, open and sheltered water. Squirrels and foxes need to drink, some insects appear to do so, and birds like to bathe as well as drink. It is vital to make special provision in times of drought – and that means in mid-winter as well as in dry summers. Heavy frosts lock up all of the free water in the environment, and birds in particular suffer if they cannot drink. Everyone can provide water – even if you live in a fifteenth floor flat you can put a pan of water on your balcony.

City wildlife parks

In the last twenty years, many abandoned or neglected pieces of land have been turned into city wildlife parks. They may have a local name, or be called community nature parks, nature gardens or ecological parks. There was a famous, ephemeral, example of the latter called the William Curtis Ecological Park, which pioneered this approach to nature conservation in urban areas. It was built on an old lorry park alongside the River Thames, opposite the Tower of London and in the shadow of Tower Bridge. It was opened in 1977 as part of the Queen's Silver Jubilee celebrations and closed in 1985, although the site has never been redeveloped. In 1980 the habitats included gorse scrub, sand dune, hedgerow, wet meadow, dry meadow, pond, cornfield, alder carr and willow bed. Three hundrd and forty-eight different kinds of plant grew there, of which 205 arrived of their own accord. Thirty-one kinds of bird were recorded, including heron, black redstart, linnet, goldcrest and partridge. Foxes and hedgehogs were visiting the park.

Now it is just another patch of close-mown grass.

Such places are usually managed by voluntary agencies with the help of local people.

The starting point may be a barren site, one with artificial features, such as a canal, reservoir or garden, one with natural features, such as a wood or pool, or a site with a combination of these. Typically half a dozen or so habitats will be present or will be introduced, often in a remarkably small space. The favourite combination is spring meadow, summer meadow, woodland and/or woodland edge, open water and marsh or bog. There is often a building with a classroom and exhibition area. Local people are encouraged to use and enjoy these places. While they do so, they are helped to appreciate and enjoy, not just the nature park itself but also the natural world in general. Schoolchildren are catered for, and a great deal of formal and informal education takes place.

Most large towns and cities now have such nature parks. Examples include:

London	Camley St Natural Park
Bristol	Willsbridge Mill
Birmingham	The Centre of the Earth
Dudley	Saltwells Wood
Grangemouth	The Jupiter Project
Manchester	Trafford Ecology Park

First aid

We have seen that towns and cities are very amenable to wildlife, but they are dangerous places as well. Apparently abandoned or injured animals, especially young birds, are frequently found. Often the greatest danger they are in is from well meaning people who try to help them!

What we think are abandoned youngsters rarely are. It is normal for fledglings to leave the nest before they can fly properly. They will shelter in undergrowth whilst their parents are away collecting their next meal, and will emerge when called by the returning adults. People in the vicinity are likely to prevent the return of the parents and terrify the youngster. Many of these young birds do become a meal for a cat, fox or bigger bird, but this is the way the world works. Their chances of survival are higher while their parents are there to look after them than if we try to do it.

You should take all this into account before taking a baby bird or animal into your care. Just picking up the youngster is likely to send it into a state of shock and panic. It may injure itself thrashing about, and it should be put into a dark, well ventilated box and transferred to somewhere quiet, warm and dry as soon as possible. All this is only half of the equation. The other half is that looking after such a youngster is very demanding. They need an almost constant supply of special food. Adult blue tits locate hundreds of caterpillars for their broods in what seems to be no time at all – see how many you can find in thirty minutes intense searching of a corner of your garden. You must identify your patient (not always easy with fledglings) and find out what it normally eats, whether insects, worms or seeds. Then you have to work out a way of supplying that food for up to eighteen hours a day.

If you are successful in raising the new addition to your family you may find that it becomes just that – an addition to the family. Young animals and birds raised by people come to think that they are people as well, and become dependant on the support and company of humans. Once this tameness develops they are most unlikely to be able to survive in the wild. Your cuddly bundle of fur which was once a fox cub can soon grow into an aggressive smelly fox which thinks your lounge and kitchen are its territory.

If the animal you have found is injured rather than apparently abandoned you have to decide on one of three courses of action – leave it to fend for itself, despatch it as humanely as possible or take it into your care.

The first will of course cause you the least trouble, except perhaps with your conscience. There is nothing wrong with doing this however. Animals have always had to face risks, have been injured, and have survived or not according to their circumstances. It may be best to exercise the second option if you think that the unfortunate creature will suffer if left alone, but that it has little chance of recovering. If you take it into your care then all the problems mentioned abov will be apparent. If your new patient is an adult you will have the added proble of protecting yourself from bites, pecks or scratches (although these risks shou not be ignored even with young animals and birds). Squirrels have sharp teet and claws, badgers have a very strong and dangerous bite, and birds of prey hav sharp talons and deadly beaks. You must take extra care to protect your ey when dealing with birds of prey.

You should not in any case attempt to treat and care for injured animals witl out taking expert advice. You should contact a vet, the RSPCA, the RSPB, th local Wildlife Trust, or a nearby nature or bird of prey centre. They will tell yo what is best for your patient. There are an increasing number of people involve in wildlife rehabilitation, and there may be someone living close to you who wi take the animal in. The specialist agencies will know if this is the case.

Wildlife and the law

There is a surprising amount of legislation relating to wildlife. Chief amongst this is the Wildlife and Countryside Act but there are a number of others, including the Abandonment of Animals Act, the Protection of Animals Act, and, in a botanical context, the Weeds Act. Birds and bats enjoy the greatest amount of favourable legislation, but the law attempts to control our relationships with almost every part of the natural world, from algae to albatrosses, and from moths to molluscs. The average city dweller is not likely to transgress the law relating to the lagoon sea slug or the fen raft spider (both protected) but if your dog enters a badger sett, or bats become your lodgers, then you will need to know the law. (In the former case you should generally allow 48 hours for the dog to emerge of its own accord, although you can make encouraging noises from the entrance. In the meantime you will need to negotiate a licence to disturb the sett, in case you need to dig your dog out, with your local office of the Ministry of Agriculture, Fisheries and Food. In the latter case you must contact your local office of English Nature if you wish to disturb the bats or their roost for any reason.)

Legislation generally requires that listed species should not be 'intentionally killed, injured or taken'; and, as with badgers and bats, the legislation can extend to protecting the places they live as well as the animals themselves. Exceptions to protection are often listed for the purposes of trade, sport, nursing, humane destruction or pest control, or in pursuit of a 'lawful activity'. Some laws relate to the prevention of cruelty or suffering, or to the release of certain species into the wild. It is, for instance, illegal to 'release' giant hogweed into the wild, although you can grow it in your garden. Another very important point about plants is that it is illegal to uproot any wild plant without the permission of the land owner, and to even pick the flowers of nearly 200 species, although none of these is likely to be found growing casually in the middle of cities.

If you take a wild creature into your care as described above you become subject to the laws regarding cruelty. Every captive animal, whether a domestic pet, a laboratory animal, a farm animal or a distressed wild animal receives legal protection from ill treatment.

A lot of common urban species are at opposite ends of the legal spectrum. So-called pest species include most of the crow family, including jays and jackdaws which seem to lead pretty innocuous lives, feral pigeons, house sparrows and starlings, foxes and grey squirrels. On the other hand bats, badgers, frogs, toads, great-crested and common newts, slow-worms and lizards are all legally protected. To avoid falling foul of the law a good general rule is: make provision for wildlife and enjoy watching it, but do not kill, capture or keep individual animals or birds.

Further Reading

Christopher Lever, *The Naturalized Animals of the British Isles* (Hutchinson, London, 1977)

Gavin Weightman and Mike Birkhead, *City Safari, Wildlife in London* (Sidgwick and Jackson, London, 1986)

E.M. Nicholson, *Birds and Men* (Collins New Naturalist, Collins, London, 1951)

C Baines, *The Wild Side of Town* (BBC Publications and Elm Tree Books, London, 1986)

C. Baines, *How to Make a Wildlife Garden* (Elm Tree Books, London, 1985)

M. Chinery and W. G. Teagle, *Wildlife in Towns and Cities* (Country Life Books, Feltham, 1985)

W. H. Hudson, *Birds in London* (Longmans Green, 1898; reprinted by David and Charles, Newton Abbot, 1969)

B. Smyth, *City Wildspace* (Hilary Shipman, London, 1987)

Stephen Harris, *Urban Foxes* (Whittet Books, London, 1986)

Michael Chinery, *Garden Creepy Crawlies* (Whittet Books, London, 1986)

Pat Morris, *Hedgehogs* (Whittet Books, London, 1983)

Index

Figures in bold indicate illustrations

The Whittet series of Natural History titles have been described as 'good, popular accounts with a well judged blend of fact, folk-myth and humour' (*Scottish Wildlife*) and 'aimed at a broad audience, light enough for the young enthusiast, yet detailed enough to satisfy any interested adult' (Hugh Warwick, *BBC Wildlife*).

Three times they have been Highly Commended in the Natural World Book Awards

If you have enjoyed this book, you might be interested in other natural history titles we publish; write for a free booklist to 18 Anley Road, London W14 OBY. You may purchase the titles below either from bookshops or direct from us. All are priced at £7.99 except where indicated, and all are illustrated with line drawings throughout. Please add £1.50 p & p when ordering direct:

World Wildlife Series

ANTS
Ray North

BIG CATS
Douglas Richardson
(£9.99)

CHIMPANZEES
Tess Lemmon

DOLPHINS
Peter Evans

DUCKS
David Tomlinson

PARROTS
David Alderton
(£9.99)

PENGUINS
John A. Love

SEA OTTERS
John A. Love
(£9.99)

SPIDERS
Michael Chinery

British Natural History Series

BADGERS
Michael Clark

BATS
Phil Richardson

DEER
Norma Chapman

EAGLES
John A. Love

FALCONS
Andrew Village

FROGS AND TOADS
Trevor Beebee

GARDEN CREEPY-CRAWLIES
Michael Chinery

HEDGEHOGS
Pat Morris

MAMMAL DETECTIVE
Rob Strachan

MICE AND VOLES
John Flowerdew

OTTERS
Paul Chanin

OWLS
Chris Mead

POND LIFE
Trevor Beebee

PONIES IN THE WILD
Elaine Gill

PUFFINS
Kenny Taylor

RABBITS AND HARES
Anne McBride

ROBINS
Chris Mead

SEALS
Sheila Anderson

SNAKES AND LIZARDS
Tom Langton

SQUIRRELS
Jessica Holm

STOATS AND WEASELS
Paddy Sleeman

Future titles include COUNTRY
FOXES and DORMICE